# SRA Reading Mastery

*Signature Edition*

## Series Guide for the Language Arts and Literature Strands

 **SRA**

*Columbus, OH*

## Acknowledgments

SRA/McGraw-Hill gratefully acknowledges the authors of the Language Arts and Literature components of *Reading Mastery Signature Edition*.

Siegfried Engelmann

Jean Osborn

Karen Lou Seitz Davis

Jerry Silbert

Bonnie Grossen

Susan Hanner

Steve Osborn

Leslie Zoref

**SRAonline.com**

 **SRA**

Send all inquiries to this address:
SRA/McGraw-Hill
4400 Easton Commons
Columbus, OH 43219

ISBN: 978-0-07-612676-7
MHID: 0-07-612676-5

3 4 5 6 7 8 9 10  WDQ  13 12 11 10

The *McGraw-Hill* Companies

# Contents

# Reading Mastery Signature Edition

*Reading Mastery Signature Edition* is the sixth edition of *Reading Mastery,* which was originally published in 1969 as *Distar Reading.* The Signature Edition greatly expands and refines the instruction found in previous editions.

## The Strands

The Signature Edition consists of three strands for students in Grades K through 5. The strands are (1) Reading and Spelling, (2) Language Arts, and (3) Literature.

The Reading and Spelling strand is scheduled daily and presents core decoding, comprehension, and spelling activities. The Language Arts strand and the Literature strand are designed to complement the Reading strand.

The Language Arts programs are strongly recommended for teachers of at-risk students in Grades K, 1, and 2. These students, particularly, need to become familiar with the language of instruction—the language they will encounter now and later in textbooks.

Neither the Language Arts strand nor the Literature strand should be scheduled as part of the daily reading periods.

All three *Reading Mastery Signature Edition* strands have clearly stated goals and objectives.

### The **Reading** strand

- addresses all five essential components of reading as identified by Reading First: phonemic awareness, phonics and word analysis, fluency, vocabulary, and comprehension.

- provides spelling instruction to help students make the connection between decoding and spelling patterns.
- develops decoding, word recognition, and comprehension skills that transfer to other subject areas.

### The **Language Arts** strand

- teaches the oral language skills necessary to understand what is said, written, and read in the classroom.
- helps students communicate ideas and information effectively.
- develops students' ability to use writing strategies and processes successfully.

### The **Literature** strand

- supports the Reading strand by offering a wide variety of literary forms and text structures.
- provides multiple opportunities for students to work with comprehension strategies and to write for authentic purposes.
- gives ample opportunity for students to read independently.

This Series Guide focuses on the Language Arts and Literature strands of *Reading Mastery Signature Edition.* The Language Arts section of this guide begins on the next page. The Literature section begins on page 117. For more information on the Reading strand, consult the *Series Guide for the Reading Strand.*

# Language Arts Strand Overview

The *Reading Mastery Signature Edition* Language Arts strand includes six year-long programs (Grades K–5). The content of each program differs, but the instructional approach is consistent throughout. Key features include

- a Direct Instruction approach for the explicit teaching of necessary language concepts, thinking skills, and writing techniques.
- daily lessons that present an organized sequence of exercises.
- teacher scripts for clear and consistent presentation of exercises in the daily lessons.
- ample opportunity for both group and individual practice with the contents of the exercises.
- continuous integration and review of all language concepts, thinking skills, and writing techniques taught earlier in the program.
- placement tests and progress assessments to ensure that students are placed in the correct program and lesson and are mastering the concepts, skills, and techniques taught in the program.

The main student and teacher materials for each grade are listed below.

| Teacher Materials | K | 1 | 2 | 3 | 4 | 5 |
|---|---|---|---|---|---|---|
| Language Arts Presentation Book(s) | ◆ | ◆ | ◆ | ◆ | ◆ | ◆ |
| Teacher's Guide | ◆ | ◆ | ◆ | ◆ | ◆ | ◆ |
| Answer Key | ◆ | ◆ | ◆ | ◆ | ◆ | ◆ |
| Student Materials | | | | | | |
| Workbook(s) | ◆ | ◆ | ◆ | ◆ | | |
| Textbook | | | ◆ | ◆ | ◆ | ◆ |

## Teacher Materials

**Language Arts Presentation Books** (Grades K–5) contain presentation scripts for every lesson. The scripts tell you what to say and do. The scripts also specify students' answers. Many scripts give specific procedures for correcting students' mistakes. Reduced student pages provide an easy reference to what students are viewing or reading.

**Teacher's Guides** (Grades K–5) explain each level in detail and provide specific teaching techniques for many types of exercises. The guides also contain correction procedures, suggestions for classroom management, placement tests, lists of objectives, and other helpful material.

**Answer Keys** (Grades K–5) contain answers for items in the student Workbooks and Textbooks.

## Student Materials

**Workbooks** (Grades K–3) are softbound consumable books containing questions and exercises that students complete during each lesson. Students write the answers to Workbook items in the Workbook.

**Textbooks** (Grades 2–5) are hardbound, full-color books containing comprehension and skill activities that students complete on lined paper.

## Lessons and Exercises

Each level of *Reading Mastery* Language Arts consists of daily lessons that you present to students. The number of lessons in each level varies, but the average is about 130 lessons per level.

A typical lesson lasts about 45 minutes and consists of a series of exercises. Each exercise teaches a specific language concept, thinking skill, or writing technique. An average lesson includes 5–10 exercises.

The exercises are both oral and written. For the oral exercises, you present questions and instructions from the Language Arts Presentation Book, and the students respond orally. For example, in Grade K Language, you ask students to perform actions and make complete statements about what they are doing. For the written exercises, students complete activities in their Workbooks or Textbooks, either under your direction or independently. In Grade 5 Language Arts, for example, students read sentences in their Textbook and write the part of speech for each word.

## Tracks

The exercises in each level of the program are organized into tracks. Each track focuses on a particular set of language concepts, thinking skills, or writing techniques. A typical lesson includes exercises from several tracks.

The exercises within a particular track appear over a span of lessons. In Grade K Language, for example, the exercises that teach days of the week appear in lessons 35–74, and the exercises that teach prepositions appear in lessons 27–88.

Tracks that teach a particular language concept, thinking skill, or writing technique are grouped with other tracks that teach related concepts or skills. For example, in Grade 4 Language Arts, the "Study Skills" group includes tracks that teach main idea, taking notes, and outlining.

The scope and sequence charts that appear later in this guide show the tracks and track groups in each level of *Reading Mastery* Language Arts. Every concept, skill, and technique introduced in the programs is consistently taught, applied, and reviewed for several lessons until students achieve mastery.

In Grades 1–5, the first time an exercise appears, the objective for that exercise is written in boldface type in the list of objectives at the beginning of the lesson.

## Patterned Exercises

Exercises within each track are formatted, or "patterned." Patterned exercises are easier for you to teach and easier for students to follow. By learning how to present one exercise of a particular type, you learn how to present similar exercises that appear in later lessons.

The exercises use the following typefaces:

- ■ What you say is in blue type:
  You say this.

- ■ What you do is enclosed in parentheses:
  (You do this.)

- ■ Student responses are in italics:
  *Students say this.*

Two patterned exercises from the Opposites track in Grade K Language appear below. In the first exercise, which appears in Lesson 86, students say the opposites of *big, old,* and *small.* In the second exercise, from Lesson 87, students say the opposites of *empty, young,* and *dry.* The items are different, but the steps for presenting each exercise are identical.

---

**Opposites** (Lesson 86)

We're going to play a word game.

a. Listen. I'm thinking about a bed that is not big. It's not big. So what do you know about it? (Pause. Signal.) *It's small.*

b. Listen. I'm thinking of turtles that are not old. They're not old. So what do you know about them? (Pause. Signal.) *They're young.*

c. Listen. I'm thinking of a hill that is not small. It's not small. So what do you know about it? (Pause. Signal.) *It's big.*

d. (Repeat the exercise until all children's responses are firm.)

---

**Opposites** (Lesson 87)

We're going to play a word game.

a. Listen. I'm thinking about a balloon that is not empty. It's not empty. So what do you know about it? (Pause. Signal.) *It's full.*

b. Listen. I'm thinking of monsters that are not young. They're not young. So what do you know about them? (Pause. Signal.) *They're old.*

c. Listen. I'm thinking of a bridge that is not dry. It's not dry. So what do you know about it? (Pause. Signal.) *It's wet.*

d. (Repeat the exercise until all children's responses are firm.)

---

Exercises that follow the same pattern allow students to learn a concept by practicing the concept with different examples. Patterns also help students realize the similarities among the various types of exercises. In addition, patterned exercises reduce the time you need to prepare for teaching the lessons.

# Grade K Language Strand

The Language strand for *Reading Mastery Signature Edition,* Grade K, contains 150 daily lessons that teach students the words, concepts, and statements important to both oral and written language. The program emphasizes language as a means of describing the world and as a tool for thinking and for solving problems. This language can be described as the language of learning and instruction.

## Materials

The following teacher and student materials are available for Grade K Language:

### Teacher Materials

- Language Presentation Books (4)
- Teacher's Guide
- Behavioral Objectives Booklet
- Skills Profile Folder
- Answer Key
- Picture Book (Assessment)

### Student Materials

- Workbooks (2)

### Comprehensive Program Materials

- *Reading Mastery Signature Edition,* Grade K Reading Strand
- *Reading Mastery Signature Edition,* Grade K Literature Strand

## Program Contents

As shown by the Scope and Sequence Chart on page 6, Grade K Language contains six groups of tracks, each of which teaches a related set of language concepts and thinking skills. Exercises from a particular group of tracks occur over a span of individual lessons.

### Actions

In the Actions exercises, students learn concepts by performing actions themselves or by describing actions shown in pictures. At first, students perform simple actions, such as standing up or touching the floor. In subsequent lessons, they learn to produce full statements that describe their actions and use the proper tense: *I am standing up; I was standing up.* They also learn the names of parts of the body *(I am touching my chin)* and the uses of various pronouns *(You are standing up; We are standing up).* Finally, students analyze a sequence of pictures that depict a person (or animal) doing different actions. Students describe what the person *is* doing, what he or she *was* doing, and what he or she *will* do.

### Descriptions of Objects

In the Descriptions of Objects exercises, students learn how to describe basic features of objects. In the early lessons, they identify pictures of common objects, such as a tree or a car. They learn how to make identity statements about pictured objects *(This is a tree)* and how to use the word *not (This is not a car).* They also identify and make statements about objects they see and use in the classroom. Next they learn how to use pairs of opposites *(long/short, wet/ dry)* to describe objects. They also practice distinguishing between singular and plural words. Finally, they compare objects by using words such as *bigger* and *smaller,* and they make statements such as *The ball is bigger than the cup.*

## Information and Background Knowledge

In the Information and Background Knowledge exercises, students learn basic information about themselves and the world. They learn the names of their teacher and school, the days of the week, and the months and seasons of the year. They also learn the names of parts of the body, as well as the names and functions of the parts of common objects. They identify the materials of which common objects are made, and they acquire background knowledge about common occupations, natural phenomena, and locations.

## Instructional Words and Problem-Solving Concepts

In the Instructional Words and Problem-Solving Concepts exercises, students learn the meanings and uses of words and concepts that are important for following instructions, solving logical problems, and answering questions. They learn that *first, next,* and *last* are words that describe both temporal events (what somebody does first) and spatial relationships (who is first in line). They also learn the prepositions *on, over, in front of, in, in back of, under, next to,* and *between,* and they use the prepositions to describe the relationship of objects in a picture *(The dog is in front of the bike).* In some exercises, students compare objects and identify features that are the same or different. They also learn the meanings of key instructional words *(and, or, some, all, none)* and they practice answering questions that begin with *where, who, when,* or *what.* Finally, in the If/Then track, they learn about deductive reasoning.

## Classification

In the Classification exercises, students learn nine classes of objects, including vehicles, food, containers, clothing, animals, buildings, plants, tools, and furniture. They also learn the names of many objects that belong to each class, and they make statements that relate objects to their class. For some classes, they learn rules, such as *A vehicle is made to take you places.* Students practice using these rules to determine whether an object is in a given class.

## Problem-Solving Strategies and Applications

Rather than teaching new concepts, the Problem-Solving Strategies and Applications exercises provide new contexts, new uses, and new statements for the concepts taught in the other tracks of the program. In a typical Concept Application exercise, students view a picture that shows different examples of an object, such as an apple. They learn a rule about one of the apples, such as *The rabbit will eat the big apple that has leaves.* After students identify which apple the rabbit will eat, they see another picture that confirms their prediction.

# Grade K Language Scope and Sequence Chart

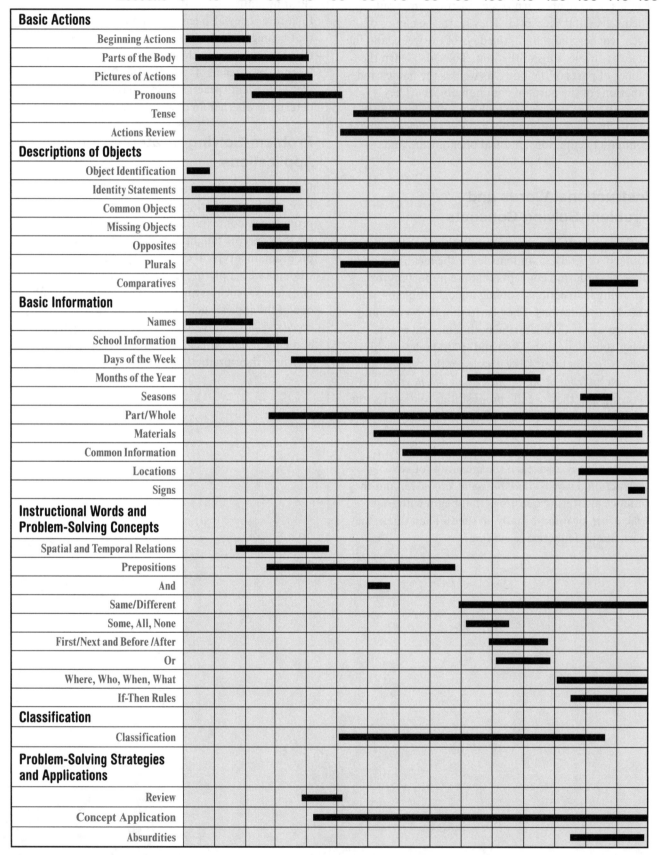

| | Lessons | 0 | 10 | 20 | 30 | 40 | 50 | 60 | 70 | 80 | 90 | 100 | 110 | 120 | 130 | 140 | 150 |
|---|---|---|---|---|---|---|---|---|---|---|---|---|---|---|---|---|---|

**Basic Actions**
- Beginning Actions
- Parts of the Body
- Pictures of Actions
- Pronouns
- Tense
- Actions Review

**Descriptions of Objects**
- Object Identification
- Identity Statements
- Common Objects
- Missing Objects
- Opposites
- Plurals
- Comparatives

**Basic Information**
- Names
- School Information
- Days of the Week
- Months of the Year
- Seasons
- Part/Whole
- Materials
- Common Information
- Locations
- Signs

**Instructional Words and Problem-Solving Concepts**
- Spatial and Temporal Relations
- Prepositions
- And
- Same/Different
- Some, All, None
- First/Next and Before /After
- Or
- Where, Who, When, What
- If-Then Rules

**Classification**
- Classification

**Problem-Solving Strategies and Applications**
- Review
- Concept Application
- Absurdities

# Grade 1 Language Arts Strand

The Language Arts strand for *Reading Mastery Signature Edition,* Grade 1, contains 130 daily lessons that emphasize language concepts, story grammar and literature, and writing. Each lesson contains several types of Language Concepts exercises. These may include classification, word skills, sentence skills, reasoning skills, directions skills, information, or applications. The Story Grammar and Literature exercises contain interesting and amusing stories that allow students to learn about character development. The exercises provide frequent opportunities for students to predict what characters will do. Using story grammar, students are able to do extension and extrapolation tasks, such as collecting data, identifying characters by what they say, completing stories, and performing plays. Finally, the Writing exercises include story-related sentence writing, cooperative story writing, main-idea sentence writing, and sequencing.

## Materials

The following teacher and student materials are available for Grade 1 Language Arts:

### Teacher Materials

- Language Arts Presentation Books (2)
- Teacher's Guide
- Answer Key

### Student Materials

- Workbook

### Comprehensive Program Materials

- *Reading Mastery Signature Edition,* Grade 1 Reading Strand
- *Reading Mastery Signature Edition,* Grade 1 Literature Strand

## Program Contents

As shown by the Scope and Sequence Chart on pages 10–11, Grade 1 Language Arts contains three main groups of tracks: language concepts, story grammar and literature, and writing. Story Grammar and Literature has two subgroups (story grammar and story completion), and Writing has three subgroups (story-related writing, main-idea sentence writing, and sequence sentence writing).

### Language Concepts

The Language Concepts group of tracks is divided into eight subgroups: actions, classification, word skills, sentence skills, reasoning skills, directional skills, information, and applications.

**Actions** The first exercise in Grade 1 Language Arts lessons is often an Actions routine in which students perform specific actions. Your questions and instructions require students to describe what they did, are doing, or will do. The concepts presented include prepositions, tense, some/all/none, same/different, and/or, and pronouns.

**Classification** The Classification track has several objectives, including

- reviewing the names of common classes, such as furniture and vehicles.
- setting the stage for definitions that involve class names.
- teaching the relationship between larger and smaller classes.
- showing how objects are the same. For example, a pair of pliers and a pencil are the same because both are tools.

**Word Skills** In the Word Skills tracks, children learn to

- name and recognize pairs of words that are opposites.
- define a word, first by naming a class for the things being defined, then by indicating characteristics of the things being defined that are true of only those things.
- identify objects that are described through clues.
- name and recognize synonyms.
- form contractions using the correct pronoun and verb forms.

**Sentence Skills** The four Sentence Skills tracks deal with the properties of sentences and set the stage for grammatical analysis. The tracks

- demonstrate that specific parts of sentences answer *who, what, when, where,* or *why* questions.
- give students practice in asking questions, discriminating between the question and the answer, and discriminating between the simple answer and the answer expressed as a complete statement.
- provide practice in transforming statements in a given tense to statements in other tenses.
- demonstrate that a particular statement is limited in what it tells about an event.

**Reasoning Skills** The tracks in the Reasoning Skills group include same/different, true/false, can do, only, descriptions, analogies, questions and clues, and if-then. All of these tracks

- deal with problem-solving. They involve relationships between objects and events rather than a single feature of an object or event.
- involve fairly complex instructions. For example, you ask, Tell me if what I say is true of **only** the boat or if it is true of the boat **and** the car. The student responses usually consist of complete statements.
- involve concepts that have already been taught. Students apply the concepts to figure out the answers to problems.

**Directional Skills** Many teaching demonstrations and worksheet instructions used in the primary grades assume that students understand the meanings of such terms as *from* and *to.* Students are also expected to be able to read and understand simple maps. The exercises in the Directional Skills track

- teach the meanings of the words *from, to, north, south, east,* and *west.*
- provide adequate practice in making statements that contain these words.

**Information** The two main Information tracks present information about calendars and common materials, such as concrete, plastic, and wood. Students also learn about the features of a particular location (such as a doctor's office or a forest) and about the parts of common objects.

**Applications** Students apply rules to different situations in the two Applications tracks: absurdities and temporal sequencing. In the absurdities track, students are first presented with situations that have a serious incongruity or inconsistency; students then identify what is absurd about the situation and tell why it is absurd. In the temporal sequencing track, students identify a sequence of events or perform a sequence of events according to verbal directions.

## Story Grammar and Literature

In Grade 1 Language Arts, children learn how to construct stories according to the constraints of different story grammars. The stories in the program are uniquely designed for this teaching, and the sequence ensures that all students learn important skills associated with stories. This knowledge sets the stage for comprehension skills that students are expected to apply in reading programs. The stories in Grade 1 Language Arts specifically address those aspects of comprehension that typically give older students trouble when reading stories.

Grade 1 Language Arts teaches students how to create parallel stories based on familiar story grammars. For this teaching, model stories are introduced. Each model has a unique story grammar. Students extrapolate the details of the model stories to create new stories with the same grammar.

Well-written stories present characters who have distinguishing features, who reason and dream, and who do things to reach goals. The stories in Grade 1 Language Arts present problems or conflicts and outcomes that are largely implied by the story details. Students focus their attention on these details and make predictions inferred from the details.

Story grammar also prepares students for writing activities. Although extensive story writing does not begin until Grade 3 Language Arts, the early work on story grammar provides students with the basic knowledge they need to be constructors of interesting stories, not merely critics or categorizers of story details. During Grade 1 Language Arts, students engage in many "construction" activities (participating in plays, making up oral stories) that require applying knowledge of story grammar.

## Writing

Grade 1 Language Arts includes several groups of Writing tracks. For story-related writing, students first assemble cut-out pictures into visual "sentences." Then they write the sentences. In later activities, students use pictures as prompts for writing sentences.

Students also write endings to stories cooperatively. After you read the first part of a story, students dictate an ending to the story, which you write on the board. Finally, students copy the ending.

For main-idea sentences, students write the main idea of a simple picture. For sequence exercises, students are presented with a sequence of pictures and write a sentence about each one.

# Grade 1 Language Arts Scope and Sequence Chart

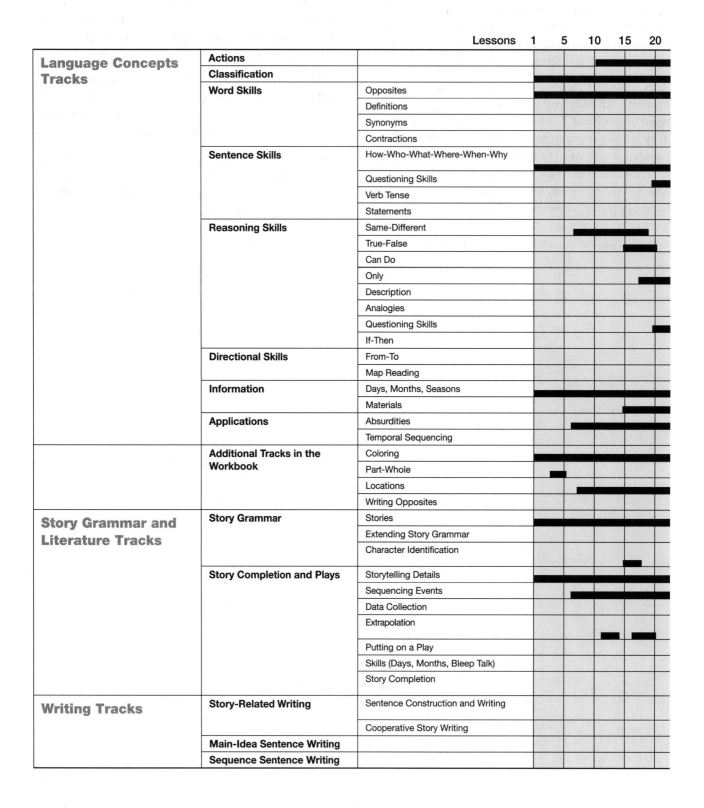

| | | Lessons | 1 | 5 | 10 | 15 | 20 |
|---|---|---|---|---|---|---|---|
| **Language Concepts Tracks** | **Actions** | | | | | | |
| | **Classification** | | | | | | |
| | **Word Skills** | Opposites | | | | | |
| | | Definitions | | | | | |
| | | Synonyms | | | | | |
| | | Contractions | | | | | |
| | **Sentence Skills** | How-Who-What-Where-When-Why | | | | | |
| | | Questioning Skills | | | | | |
| | | Verb Tense | | | | | |
| | | Statements | | | | | |
| | **Reasoning Skills** | Same-Different | | | | | |
| | | True-False | | | | | |
| | | Can Do | | | | | |
| | | Only | | | | | |
| | | Description | | | | | |
| | | Analogies | | | | | |
| | | Questioning Skills | | | | | |
| | | If-Then | | | | | |
| | **Directional Skills** | From-To | | | | | |
| | | Map Reading | | | | | |
| | **Information** | Days, Months, Seasons | | | | | |
| | | Materials | | | | | |
| | **Applications** | Absurdities | | | | | |
| | | Temporal Sequencing | | | | | |
| | **Additional Tracks in the Workbook** | Coloring | | | | | |
| | | Part-Whole | | | | | |
| | | Locations | | | | | |
| | | Writing Opposites | | | | | |
| **Story Grammar and Literature Tracks** | **Story Grammar** | Stories | | | | | |
| | | Extending Story Grammar | | | | | |
| | | Character Identification | | | | | |
| | **Story Completion and Plays** | Storytelling Details | | | | | |
| | | Sequencing Events | | | | | |
| | | Data Collection | | | | | |
| | | Extrapolation | | | | | |
| | | Putting on a Play | | | | | |
| | | Skills (Days, Months, Bleep Talk) | | | | | |
| | | Story Completion | | | | | |
| **Writing Tracks** | **Story-Related Writing** | Sentence Construction and Writing | | | | | |
| | | Cooperative Story Writing | | | | | |
| | **Main-Idea Sentence Writing** | | | | | | |
| | **Sequence Sentence Writing** | | | | | | |

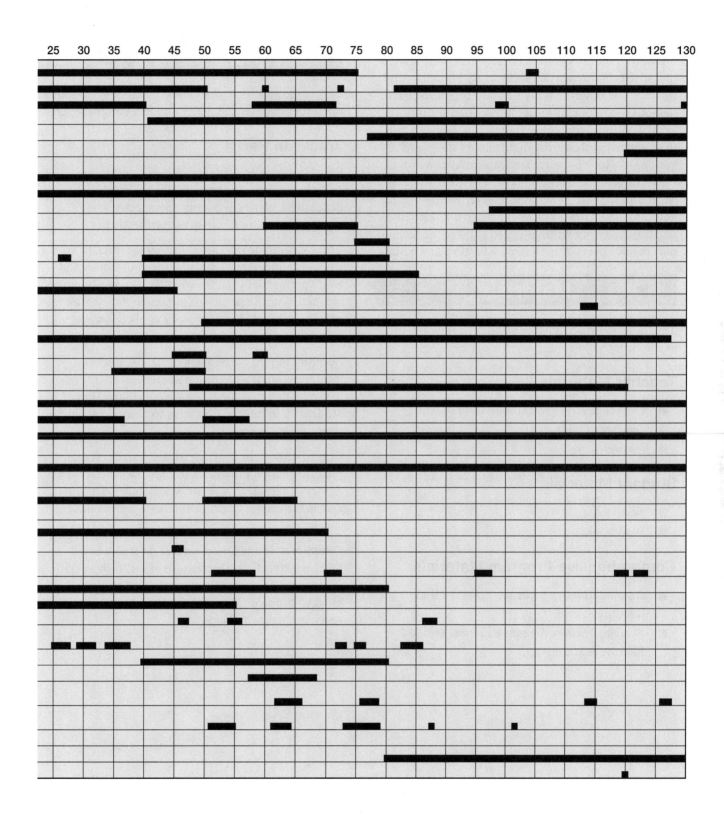

# Grade 2 Language Arts Strand

The Language Arts strand for *Reading Mastery Signature Edition,* Grade 2, contains 110 daily lessons that teach comprehension skills, story grammar, and writing. The program is divided into two parts. Part 1 (lessons 1–65) focuses on comprehension skills (such as formulating deductions, finding ambiguous words in sentences, and classification) and on story grammar, which prepares students for later writing. Part 2 (lessons 66–110) emphasizes writing. Students learn how to write paragraphs that tell the main idea and supporting details of what occurred in a given illustration. Other writing-related skills in the second part include parts of speech, punctuation, and editing.

## Materials

The following teacher and student materials are available for Grade 2:

### Teacher Materials

- Language Arts Presentation Books (2)
- Teacher's Guide
- Answer Key

### Student Materials

- Textbook
- Workbook

### Comprehensive Program Materials

- *Reading Mastery Signature Edition,* Grade 2 Reading Strand
- *Reading Mastery Signature Edition,* Grade 2 Literature Strand

## Program Contents

The Scope and Sequence Chart on pages 14–15 shows the tracks in parts 1 and 2 of Grade 2 Language Arts.

### Tracks in Part 1

Part 1 contains ten main tracks: story grammar, sequencing, classification, directions, dialect, deductions, clarity, reporting, perspectives, and writing. The main tracks are described below.

**Story Grammar** The Story Grammar track helps students anticipate what will happen in stories and relate events that occur to what they know about the characters or the situations presented. Story grammar provides opportunities for story application and extrapolation.

**Sequencing** In the Sequencing track, students interpret a static illustration as an event that is related to events that preceded it and events that follow. Students also interpret pictures to place events in temporal sequence.

**Classification** In the Classification track, students use information provided through clues to identify mystery characters or mystery sequences. Students also make classes larger or smaller by manipulating subclasses.

**Directions** In the Directions track, students follow precise instructions that involve maps, such as "Go four blocks north; turn to the west and go three blocks." Students also write instructions for getting to specified places on maps.

**Deductions** For the Deductions track, students learn how to draw a conclusion from properly presented facts. Students also identify deductions that are formally incorrect.

**Clarity** In the Clarity track, students correct vague pronouns in passages such as "The bugs were in the bushes. *They* were red." Students identify the "unclear" word and translate the possible meanings into concrete images. (One picture has bugs that are red; the other has bushes that are red.)

**Perspectives** In the Perspectives track, activities involving relative size and relative direction give students practice at viewing things from different perspectives.

**Writing** In the Writing track, students write parallel sentences based on an illustration, write about story characters, complete deductions, write letters, and alphabetize words.

## Tracks in Part 2

Part 2 of Grade 2 Language Arts teaches component skills that students need to organize and write basic passages, including main idea, reporting, clarity, passage organization, and editing.

**Main Idea** For the simplest writing assignments, students name the character in a picture and tell the main thing the character did. For these assignments, students discriminate between "the main thing the character did" and some ancillary action.

**Reporting** In the Reporting track, students are first presented with a picture and a series of statements. Students identify which statements "report" on what the picture shows, and which statements don't. Subsequently, students write their own reports about what pictures show. Instead of "making up" scenarios about what happened, students describe what the characters in the picture did.

**Clarity** The Clarity activities focus on the idea that what somebody writes may be clear to the writer but not to the reader. The initial exercises present a group of similar pictures and a group of sentences. Students identify the sentences that tell about more than one picture and the sentences that tell about only one picture. In later exercises, students identify vague words in a passage and replace them with more precise terms.

**Passage Organization** In the Passage Organization track, students are introduced to different ways of organizing passages. The simplest organization involves writing more than one sentence about a character in a picture: The first sentence tells the main thing the character did, and the following sentences provide details. In subsequent exercises, students are presented with pictures that show groups of characters doing a common activity, such as cleaning a room. No two characters are doing the same thing, but all are engaged in the "main" activity of cleaning the room. Students start with a statement about what the group did; then they write about what each individual did.

**Editing** The Editing activities are coordinated with the writing assignments so that students are not required to apply a particular rule, procedure, or skill until they have edited passages for violations of the rule, procedure, or skill. Students also edit their own writing through a series of checks. For example, after writing sentences that tell the main things characters did, students apply these checks:

- Does each sentence begin with a capital letter and end with a period?
- Does each sentence tell the main thing?
- Does each sentence tell what somebody or something did?

For many students, editing their own work is a difficult process. That's why they first learn particular skills in isolation, then edit someone else's writing, and finally edit their own writing.

# Grade 2 Language Arts Scope and Sequence Chart

**Part 1 (lessons 1–65)**

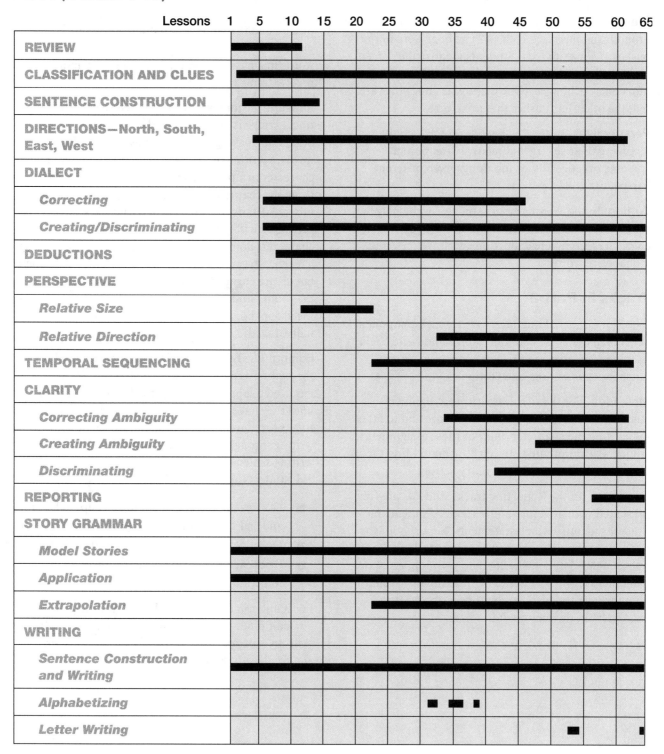

| Lessons | 1 | 5 | 10 | 15 | 20 | 25 | 30 | 35 | 40 | 45 | 50 | 55 | 60 | 65 |
|---|---|---|---|---|---|---|---|---|---|---|---|---|---|---|
| **REVIEW** | ████████████████ | | | | | | | | | | | | | |
| **CLASSIFICATION AND CLUES** | ██████████████████████████████████████████████████████████████ | | | | | | | | | | | | | |
| **SENTENCE CONSTRUCTION** | ████████████████ | | | | | | | | | | | | | |
| **DIRECTIONS—North, South, East, West** | | █████████████████████████████████████████████████████████ | | | | | | | | | | | | |
| **DIALECT** | | | | | | | | | | | | | | |
| *Correcting* | | ████████████████████████████████████████████ | | | | | | | | | | | |
| *Creating/Discriminating* | | ██████████████████████████████████████████████████████████ | | | | | | | | | | | |
| **DEDUCTIONS** | | ███████████████████████████████████████████████████████ | | | | | | | | | | | |
| **PERSPECTIVE** | | | | | | | | | | | | | | |
| *Relative Size* | | | ███████████████ | | | | | | | | | | |
| *Relative Direction* | | | | | | | ██████████████████████████████ | | | | | | |
| **TEMPORAL SEQUENCING** | | | | | | █████████████████████████████████████████████ | | | | | | |
| **CLARITY** | | | | | | | | | | | | | | |
| *Correcting Ambiguity* | | | | | | | ████████████████████████████ | | | | | |
| *Creating Ambiguity* | | | | | | | | | | ████████████████████ | | |
| *Discriminating* | | | | | | | | | █████████████████████████ | | |
| **REPORTING** | | | | | | | | | | | | ████████ | |
| **STORY GRAMMAR** | | | | | | | | | | | | | | |
| *Model Stories* | ████████████████████████████████████████████████████████████ | | | | | | | | | | | | |
| *Application* | ████████████████████████████████████████████████████████████ | | | | | | | | | | | | |
| *Extrapolation* | | | | | | ████████████████████████████████████████ | | | | | | |
| **WRITING** | | | | | | | | | | | | | | |
| *Sentence Construction and Writing* | ████████████████████████████████████████████████████████████ | | | | | | | | | | | | |
| *Alphabetizing* | | | | | | | ▪ ▪ ▪ | | | | | | |
| *Letter Writing* | | | | | | | | | | | ▪ | ▪ |

# Part 2 (lessons 66–110)

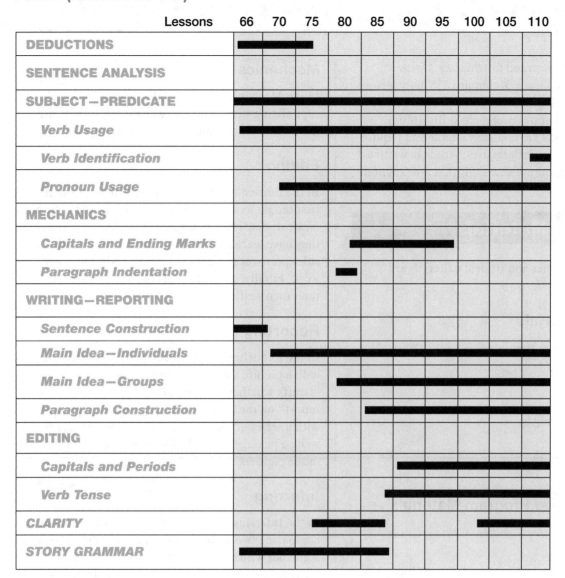

| Lessons | 66 | 70 | 75 | 80 | 85 | 90 | 95 | 100 | 105 | 110 |
|---|---|---|---|---|---|---|---|---|---|---|
| **DEDUCTIONS** | ██████████ | | | | | | | | | |
| **SENTENCE ANALYSIS** | | | | | | | | | | |
| **SUBJECT–PREDICATE** | ████████████████████████████ | | | | | | | | | |
| *Verb Usage* | ████████████████████████████ | | | | | | | | | |
| *Verb Identification* | | | | | | | | | | █ |
| *Pronoun Usage* | | ████████████████████████ | | | | | | | | |
| **MECHANICS** | | | | | | | | | | |
| *Capitals and Ending Marks* | | | | ████████████ | | | | | | |
| *Paragraph Indentation* | | | | █ | | | | | | |
| **WRITING–REPORTING** | | | | | | | | | | |
| *Sentence Construction* | ███ | | | | | | | | | |
| *Main Idea–Individuals* | | ██████████████████████████ | | | | | | | | |
| *Main Idea–Groups* | | | | ████████████████████ | | | | | | |
| *Paragraph Construction* | | | | | ██████████████████ | | | | | |
| **EDITING** | | | | | | | | | | |
| *Capitals and Periods* | | | | | | ██████████████ | | | | |
| *Verb Tense* | | | | | | █████████████████ | | | | |
| **CLARITY** | | | ████████ | | | | ████████ | | | |
| **STORY GRAMMAR** | ████████████████████ | | | | | | | | | |

# Grade 3 Language Arts Strand

The Language Arts strand for *Reading Mastery Signature Edition,* Grade 3, contains 135 daily lessons that focus on writing. The program teaches writing as a process that integrates pretaught skills. Initial writing assignments are relatively simple and require only basic sentences. Progressive changes in writing assignments incorporate new skills that are taught in the program.

## Materials

The following teacher and student materials are available for Grade 3:

### Teacher Materials

- Language Arts Presentation Books (2)
- Teacher's Guide
- Answer Key

### Student Materials

- Textbook
- Workbook

### Comprehensive Program Materials

- *Reading Mastery Signature Edition,* Grade 3 Reading Strand
- *Reading Mastery Signature Edition,* Grade 3 Literature Strand

## Program Contents

The Scope and Sequence Chart on page 18 shows the tracks in Grade 3 Language Arts. The main tracks are sentence analysis, mechanics, editing, reporting, inferring, clarity, expanded writing, resource materials, word analysis, and study skills.

### Sentence Analysis

In the Sentence Analysis tracks, students learn to identify the subject and predicate of declarative sentences; one- and two-word verbs; and pronouns, nouns, and adjectives. The exercises show students how to distinguish one part of speech from another and how to use sentence analysis when writing.

### Mechanics

In the Mechanics tracks, students learn basic rules for capitalizing words and using end marks. They also learn rules for commas, quotes, and apostrophes.

### Editing

In the Editing track, each editing skill or convention is first taught as a relatively simple rule or procedure. Next, students edit passages for violations of the rules they have learned. This practice in applying editing rules prepares students to read and edit their own work. Finally, students apply the rules while editing their own writing.

### Reporting

In the Reporting track, students are first presented with a picture and a series of statements. Students identify whether the statements "report" or "do not report" on the picture. Later, students are presented with a series of pictures that tell a story. Students write a passage that tells about the sequence of events in the pictures.

### Inferring

In the Inferring track, students draw inferences by comparing two pictures. Both pictures show the same scene but with some differences. At first, students identify how things changed from one picture to another and write sentences to describe how that change occurred. Later, students are presented with a sequence of pictures, one of which is blank. Students write a paragraph that tells what probably happened in the blank picture.

### Clarity

The two main skills emphasized in the Clarity track are (1) describing the details that distinguish one thing from similar objects and (2) using more specific words instead of general words. The basic rationale for including specific details is to give the reader a clear picture of the event or object being described.

## Expanded Writing

In the Expanded Writing track, students write stories by using what they have learned about drawing inferences, paragraphing, and rewriting. Students work on a particular story for two lessons. For some assignments, students write endings to stories that you read. For other assignments, students infer what must have happened before the events shown in an illustration.

## Resource Materials

In the Resource Materials track, students practice alphabetizing words and learn how to use indexes, glossaries, tables of contents, and dictionaries.

## Word Analysis

In the Word Analysis track, students learn about affixes, root words, compound words, and multiple meanings. They also study idiomatic expressions, similes, metaphors, and alliterations.

## Study Skills

In the Study Skills track, students learn how to make outlines. Students identify the main ideas of a given topic and then construct an outline that lists the supporting details for each main idea.

# Grade 3 Language Arts Scope and Sequence Chart

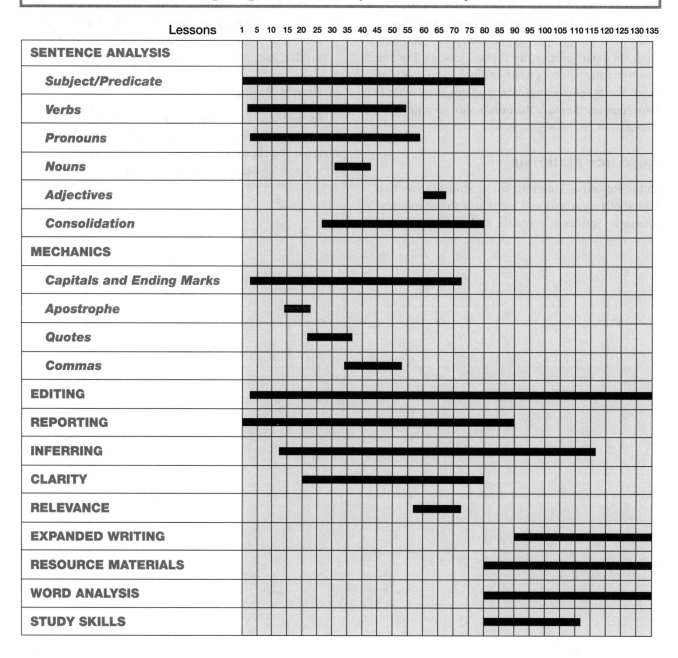

| Lessons | 1 | 5 | 10 | 15 | 20 | 25 | 30 | 35 | 40 | 45 | 50 | 55 | 60 | 65 | 70 | 75 | 80 | 85 | 90 | 95 | 100 | 105 | 110 | 115 | 120 | 125 | 130 | 135 |
|---|---|---|---|---|---|---|---|---|---|---|---|---|---|---|---|---|---|---|---|---|---|---|---|---|---|---|---|---|
| **SENTENCE ANALYSIS** | | | | | | | | | | | | | | | | | | | | | | | | | | | | |
| Subject/Predicate | | ━━━━━━━━━━━━━━━━━━━━━ | | | | | | | | | | | | | | | | | | | | | | | | | | |
| Verbs | ━━━━━━━━━━━━━━ | | | | | | | | | | | | | | | | | | | | | | | | | | | |
| Pronouns | ━━━━━━━━━━━━━━ | | | | | | | | | | | | | | | | | | | | | | | | | | | |
| Nouns | | | | | | ━━━ | | | | | | | | | | | | | | | | | | | | | | |
| Adjectives | | | | | | | | | | | ━ | | | | | | | | | | | | | | | | | |
| Consolidation | | | | | | ━━━━━━━━━━━ | | | | | | | | | | | | | | | | | | | | | |
| **MECHANICS** | | | | | | | | | | | | | | | | | | | | | | | | | | | | |
| Capitals and Ending Marks | ━━━━━━━━━━━━━━━━━━ | | | | | | | | | | | | | | | | | | | | | | | | | | | |
| Apostrophe | | ━ | | | | | | | | | | | | | | | | | | | | | | | | | | |
| Quotes | | | | ━━━ | | | | | | | | | | | | | | | | | | | | | | | | |
| Commas | | | | | | ━━━ | | | | | | | | | | | | | | | | | | | | | | |
| **EDITING** | ━━━━━━━━━━━━━━━━━━━━━━━━━━━━━━━━━━ | | | | | | | | | | | | | | | | | | | | | | | | | | | |
| **REPORTING** | ━━━━━━━━━━━━━━━━━━━━━━━ | | | | | | | | | | | | | | | | | | | | | | | | | | | |
| **INFERRING** | | | ━━━━━━━━━━━━━━━━━━━━━━━━━━━ | | | | | | | | | | | | | | | | | | | | | | | | |
| **CLARITY** | | | | ━━━━━━━━━━━━━━━ | | | | | | | | | | | | | | | | | | | | | | | |
| **RELEVANCE** | | | | | | | | | | | ━━━ | | | | | | | | | | | | | | | | | |
| **EXPANDED WRITING** | | | | | | | | | | | | | | | | | ━━━━━━━━━━━ | | | | | | | | | | |
| **RESOURCE MATERIALS** | | | | | | | | | | | | | | | | ━━━━━━━━━━━ | | | | | | | | | | | |
| **WORD ANALYSIS** | | | | | | | | | | | | | | | | ━━━━━━━━━━━ | | | | | | | | | | | |
| **STUDY SKILLS** | | | | | | | | | | | | | | | | ━━━━━━━ | | | | | | | | | | | |

# Grade 4 Language Arts Strand

The Language Arts strand for *Reading Mastery Signature Edition,* Grade 4, contains 140 daily lessons that teach expository and narrative writing, grammar, critical thinking, and study skills. The program has two parts. Part 1 (lessons 1–110) focuses on critical analysis of arguments and claims and on analyzing and correcting problems caused by lack of specificity. Part 2 (lessons 111–140) focuses on writing stories and reports, giving speeches, and using reference materials.

## Materials

The following teacher and student materials are available for Grade 4:

### Teacher Materials

- Language Arts Presentation Book
- Teacher's Guide
- Answer Key

### Student Materials

- Textbook

### Comprehensive Program Materials

- *Reading Mastery Signature Edition,* Grade 4 Reading Strand
- *Reading Mastery Signature Edition,* Grade 4 Literature Strand

## Program Contents

The Scope and Sequence Chart on pages 22–23 shows the tracks in parts 1 and 2 of Grade 4 Language Arts.

### Tracks in Part 1

The main tracks in Part 1 are parts of speech and sentence analysis, clarity, sentence types, inaccurate and unclear directions, misleading and inaccurate claims, arguments, and passage writing.

**Parts of Speech and Sentence Analysis** The Parts of Speech and Sentence Analysis tracks teach subject/predicate, verbs, nouns, pronouns, adjectives, and verb agreement. Students learn parts of speech in the context of regular-order sentences (subject-predicate order). In those sentences, the last word of the subject is either a pronoun or a noun, and the first word of the predicate is usually a verb. Adjectives come before nouns and tell about nouns. Later, students learn that a verb agrees in number with its subject. Students also learn how to move part of the predicate in front of the subject.

**Clarity** The focus of the Clarity track is on writing clear sentences. Students write directions for creating simple figures and for going places on maps. They also identify and rewrite vague pronouns in sentences, and they indicate whether statements are general or specific. Finally, students use what they have learned about clarity to write precise descriptions.

**Sentence Types** In the Sentence Types track, students work with combined sentences, compound sentences, summary sentences, and sentences that make comparisons. The work with sentence types gives students practice in expressing complex ideas. The exercises also prepare students for the extended writing activities that appear later in the program.

**Inaccurate and Unclear Directions** In the Inaccurate and Unclear Directions track, students learn that directions may be too general or inaccurate. In early exercises, students are presented with a simple figure, such as a one-inch horizontal line, and a too-general direction for drawing that figure, such as "Draw a horizontal line." Students use an "X box" (a kind of outline diagram) to identify the problem with the direction and indicate how to fix the direction: *The direction indicates that you should make a horizontal line, but that direction is too general. You should draw a horizontal line that is one inch long.* In later exercises, students construct directions for making complex figures and for traveling from one area to another.

**Misleading and Inaccurate Claims** In the Misleading and Inaccurate Claims track, students use "X boxes" to identify the problems with misleading and inaccurate claims and indicate how to fix the problems. Students first work with simple statements, then in later assignments read advertisements and find the claims that are misleading or inaccurate. In an early exercise, students are presented with claims and facts. They use "X boxes" to write explanations that indicate the problem, such as *Claim 1 states that a Dino battery gives you power hour after hour, but that claim is misleading. Dino batteries give you power for only two hours.*

**Arguments** In the Arguments track, students analyze and describe problems with arguments. The problems include irrelevant evidence, false dilemmas, and conclusions that do not follow from the evidence presented. In one lesson, for example, students read this faulty argument: "You should vacation in a place with sandy beaches. Florida is a place with sandy beaches. Therefore, you should vacation in Florida." Students write a rebuttal to the argument, such as *The argument concludes that you should vacation in Florida. Other conclusions are possible because Florida is not the only place with sandy beaches. California is a place with sandy beaches. Therefore, you could vacation in California.*

**Passage Writing** In the Passage Writing track, narrative writing exercises similar to those in Grade 3 are reviewed. Students report on pictures showing a sequence and infer what events must have happened between the pictures. In an early exercise, students write a three-paragraph passage about how a character solved a problem. The first paragraph describes the problem, the second tells what the character did to solve the problem, and the third explains the solution. In later lessons, a number of passage-writing exercises are presented in which students write extended critiques of advertisements, accounts, and editorials. Students organize the passages logically. For example, in an exercise in which students critique an advertisement with multiple misleading and inaccurate claims, students begin by summarizing the problems. Then students write separate paragraphs about the misleading claims and the inaccurate claims. Some of these critiques are in the form of letters.

## Tracks in Part 2

The tracks in Part 2 of Grade 4 Language Arts focus on writing stories and reports, giving speeches, using reference materials, and reviewing study skills. Some type of writing or speaking exercise appears in every lesson, as do exercises involving reference materials or study skills. The remaining exercises provide instruction in vocabulary development, punctuation, and grammar.

**Writing and Speaking** Students begin the Writing and Speaking track by writing stories on given topics. Students are provided with the title of the story and with directions for describing the setting and the action. In later lessons, students are presented with a picture and a set of facts or questions. They use the facts or questions to write a story about the picture. Students also write stories from different characters' perspectives.

For the Speaking exercises, students first write a five-paragraph persuasive report on a given topic. The report describes an idea, gives three specific reasons to support the idea, and then summarizes the reasons. After students finish their reports, they present them to the class as a speech. Other students take notes on the speech and discuss its strengths and weaknesses.

**Reference Materials** In the Reference Materials track, students learn about the parts of a textbook (table of contents, glossary, index) and how to use dictionaries, encyclopedias, and atlases, in both print and electronic forms. Students practice looking up words in dictionaries and using encyclopedias and atlases to answer research questions.

**Study Skills** In the Study Skills track, students identify the main idea of a passage, take notes on verbal presentations, write outlines, distinguish fact from opinion, and identify cause and effect. In a typical main-idea exercise, students write a main idea and three supporting details. In the note-taking exercise, students take notes on a passage you read aloud. They then use their notes to rewrite the passage.

**Vocabulary** In the Vocabulary track, students use different strategies to extend and improve their vocabulary. They review common prefixes and suffixes and practice attaching them to root words. They use a dictionary to look up different meanings of homographs, and they identify the meanings of common idioms and compound words. They also practice using figurative language, such as similes and metaphors. Finally, they learn how to use context clues, antonyms, and synonyms to determine the meaning of unfamiliar words.

**Punctuation and Grammar** The Punctuation and Grammar track in Part 2 expands and extends skills presented in Part 1, including parts of speech, subject/predicate, subject/verb agreement, commas, and capitalization. New exercises in Part 2 focus on sentence fragments, verb tense, contractions, and possessives.

**Part 1 (lessons 1–110)**

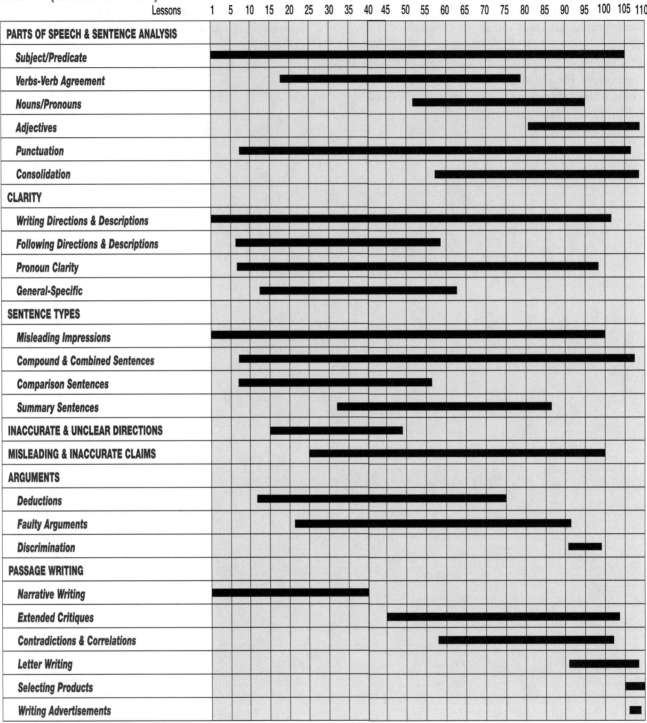

| Lessons | 1 | 5 | 10 | 15 | 20 | 25 | 30 | 35 | 40 | 45 | 50 | 55 | 60 | 65 | 70 | 75 | 80 | 85 | 90 | 95 | 100 | 105 | 110 |
|---|---|---|---|---|---|---|---|---|---|---|---|---|---|---|---|---|---|---|---|---|---|---|---|

**PARTS OF SPEECH & SENTENCE ANALYSIS**
- Subject/Predicate
- Verbs-Verb Agreement
- Nouns/Pronouns
- Adjectives
- Punctuation
- Consolidation

**CLARITY**
- Writing Directions & Descriptions
- Following Directions & Descriptions
- Pronoun Clarity
- General-Specific

**SENTENCE TYPES**
- Misleading Impressions
- Compound & Combined Sentences
- Comparison Sentences
- Summary Sentences

**INACCURATE & UNCLEAR DIRECTIONS**

**MISLEADING & INACCURATE CLAIMS**

**ARGUMENTS**
- Deductions
- Faulty Arguments
- Discrimination

**PASSAGE WRITING**
- Narrative Writing
- Extended Critiques
- Contradictions & Correlations
- Letter Writing
- Selecting Products
- Writing Advertisements

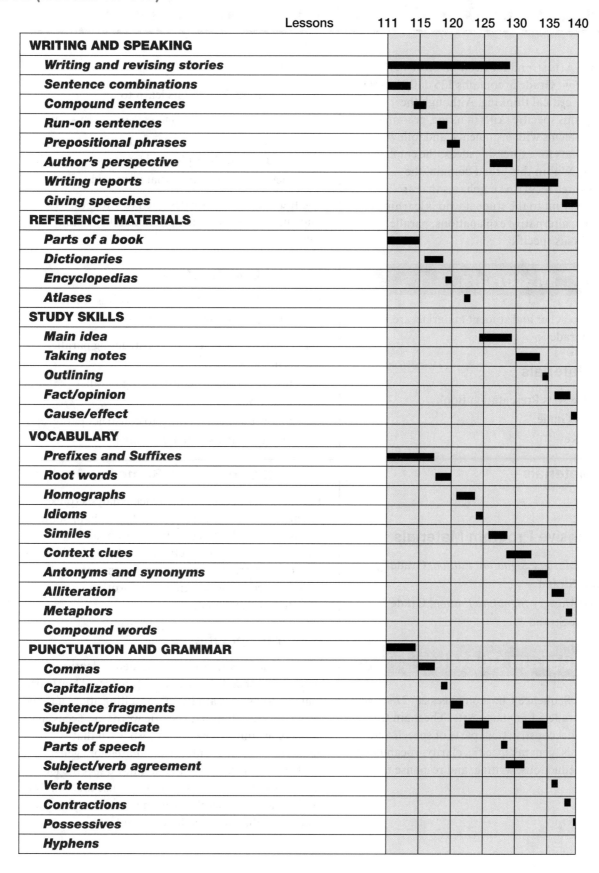

| Lessons | 111 | 115 | 120 | 125 | 130 | 135 | 140 |
|---|---|---|---|---|---|---|---|
| **WRITING AND SPEAKING** | | | | | | | |
| *Writing and revising stories* | ███████████████ | | | | | | |
| *Sentence combinations* | ██ | | | | | | |
| *Compound sentences* | | ██ | | | | | |
| *Run-on sentences* | | | ██ | | | | |
| *Prepositional phrases* | | | | ██ | | | |
| *Author's perspective* | | | | | ███ | | |
| *Writing reports* | | | | | | ███ | |
| *Giving speeches* | | | | | | | ██ |
| **REFERENCE MATERIALS** | | | | | | | |
| *Parts of a book* | ███ | | | | | | |
| *Dictionaries* | | ██ | | | | | |
| *Encyclopedias* | | | ■ | | | | |
| *Atlases* | | | | ■ | | | |
| **STUDY SKILLS** | | | | | | | |
| *Main idea* | | | | ███ | | | |
| *Taking notes* | | | | | ███ | | |
| *Outlining* | | | | | | ■ | |
| *Fact/opinion* | | | | | | | ██ |
| *Cause/effect* | | | | | | | ■ |
| **VOCABULARY** | | | | | | | |
| *Prefixes and Suffixes* | ███ | | | | | | |
| *Root words* | | ██ | | | | | |
| *Homographs* | | | ██ | | | | |
| *Idioms* | | | | ■ | | | |
| *Similes* | | | | ███ | | | |
| *Context clues* | | | | | ██ | | |
| *Antonyms and synonyms* | | | | | ███ | | |
| *Alliteration* | | | | | | ██ | |
| *Metaphors* | | | | | | | ■ |
| *Compound words* | | | | | | | |
| **PUNCTUATION AND GRAMMAR** | | | | | | | |
| *Commas* | | ██ | | | | | |
| *Capitalization* | | | ■ | | | | |
| *Sentence fragments* | | | ██ | | | | |
| *Subject/predicate* | | | | ██ | | ███ | |
| *Parts of speech* | | | | | ■ | | |
| *Subject/verb agreement* | | | | | ██ | | |
| *Verb tense* | | | | | | ■ | |
| *Contractions* | | | | | | | ■ |
| *Possessives* | | | | | | | █ |
| *Hyphens* | | | | | | | |

# Grade 5 Language Arts Strand

The Language Arts strand for *Reading Mastery Signature Edition,* Grade 5, contains 125 daily lessons that emphasize critical thinking. Although the program develops specific skills in usage, grammar, identifying problems with arguments, and following particular formats for expressing ideas, the emphasis is on thinking. Within this broad domain, the program has three recurring emphases that are particularly relevant to the student who is learning to think critically: alternative explanations, parallelism, and general versus specific.

## Materials

The following teacher and student materials are available for Grade 5:

### Teacher Materials

- Language Arts Presentation Book
- Teacher's Guide
- Answer Key

### Student Materials

- Textbook

### Comprehensive Program Materials

- *Reading Mastery Signature Edition,* Grade 5 Reading Strand
- *Reading Mastery Signature Edition,* Grade 5 Literature Strand

## Program Contents

The Scope and Sequence Chart on pages 26–27 shows the tracks in Grade 5 Language Arts. The main tracks are retell, parallel construction, parts of speech and sentence analysis, general/specific, clarity, vocabulary, descriptions, deductions, writing, and response to literature.

### Retell

In the Retell track, students learn to

- remember details of what is presented orally.
- organize information around different category headings, such as physical features and location.
- reconstruct sentences that were said.

The Retell activities are designed to strengthen students' awareness of details and ability to take notes.

### Parallel Construction

The Parallel Construction track involves several different types of exercises. Students

- test parts of speech by constructing parallel sentences.
- test directions by constructing parallel directions.
- follow outline diagrams to construct paragraphs and arguments that are parallel.

### Parts of Speech and Sentence Analysis

The Parts of Speech and Sentence Analysis track teaches and reviews many parts of speech, including nouns, verbs, adjectives, adverbs, pronouns, prepositions, and conjunctions. Students also identify subjects and predicates, convert statements into questions, combine sentences, and work on subject/verb agreement.

### General/Specific

In the General/Specific track, students identify general and specific words and sentences. They learn that general words are useful for telling about a range of possibilities, but that specific words are necessary to make meanings clear. They also learn that deductions include sentences that are more general (such as rules) and those that are more specific (such as conclusions). Eventually, students use their analysis of specific and general words and sentences to critique arguments that have inadequate evidence.

## Clarity

The Clarity track involves several different types of exercises. Students

- correct sentences with unclear pronouns *(I met Mary and her mother, and I liked her)*.
- correct statements that use the words *this* or *that* without a noun *(That made her mad)*.
- rewrite sentences so they have only the intended meaning and not a second, unintended meaning *(They watched geese fly from their yard)*.
- rewrite directions so they are clear.

## Vocabulary

In the Vocabulary track, students learn many new words. Some of these words use affixes *(misleading, unreasonable)*, some are related nouns and verbs *(achieve, achievement)*, and some can substitute for words students already know *(flood/inundate, difficult/arduous)*. Each word is introduced in context within a passage that strongly suggests the word's meaning. Students first identify a meaning that is consistent with the context, then check the dictionary to confirm the meaning. On lessons that follow the introduction of a word, students write parallel sentences that incorporate the new word.

## Descriptions

In the Descriptions track, students practice writing descriptions that are precise and clear. In a typical exercise, students view a drawing of different objects. They describe one of the objects by making only positive statements about the attributes of the object. Each sentence that provides such information rules out one or more of the other objects. When the description is completed, the sentences have ruled out all the objects except the targeted object.

## Deductions

The Deductions track involves various activities. Students

- write conclusions for deductions such as "Japan is an industrial country. All industrial countries have factories." Students write *Therefore, Japan has factories.*
- complete deductions with missing premises such as "All students study. Therefore, Fran Johnson studies." Students write *Fran Johnson is a student.*
- identify different types of faulty deductions and explain why they're faulty.
- use if-then rules to draw conclusions.

## Writing

In the Writing track, students use outline diagrams to critique various types of faulty arguments. The diagrams provide model sentences for expressing different ideas. For example, when students are presented with an inaccurate statement like "Only girls go to school," they use the outline diagram to produce a rebuttal, such as *The statement says that only girls go to school. That statement is inaccurate. Boys also go to school.*

The types of faulty arguments that students address include inaccurate statements, misleading claims, contradictions, inadequate evidence, arguments with conclusions that are too general, false cause, faulty hypothesis, and improbable inferences. For each type of faulty argument, students use an outline diagram to describe the problem with the argument.

## Response to Literature

In the Response to Literature track, students work with a short story for two lessons. During the first lesson, students read the story, write answers to literal questions about the story, and identify which paragraph of the story answers each question. During the second lesson, students write answers to interpretive questions about the story.

# Grade 5 Language Arts Scope and Sequence Chart

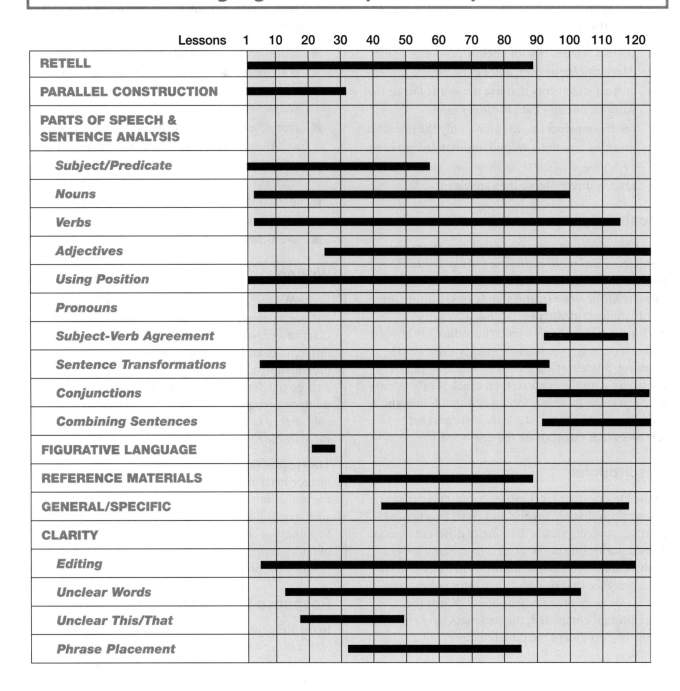

| Lessons | 1 | 10 | 20 | 30 | 40 | 50 | 60 | 70 | 80 | 90 | 100 | 110 | 120 |
|---|---|---|---|---|---|---|---|---|---|---|---|---|---|
| **RETELL** | | | | | | | | | | | | | |
| **PARALLEL CONSTRUCTION** | | | | | | | | | | | | | |
| **PARTS OF SPEECH & SENTENCE ANALYSIS** | | | | | | | | | | | | | |
| *Subject/Predicate* | | | | | | | | | | | | | |
| *Nouns* | | | | | | | | | | | | | |
| *Verbs* | | | | | | | | | | | | | |
| *Adjectives* | | | | | | | | | | | | | |
| *Using Position* | | | | | | | | | | | | | |
| *Pronouns* | | | | | | | | | | | | | |
| *Subject-Verb Agreement* | | | | | | | | | | | | | |
| *Sentence Transformations* | | | | | | | | | | | | | |
| *Conjunctions* | | | | | | | | | | | | | |
| *Combining Sentences* | | | | | | | | | | | | | |
| **FIGURATIVE LANGUAGE** | | | | | | | | | | | | | |
| **REFERENCE MATERIALS** | | | | | | | | | | | | | |
| **GENERAL/SPECIFIC** | | | | | | | | | | | | | |
| **CLARITY** | | | | | | | | | | | | | |
| *Editing* | | | | | | | | | | | | | |
| *Unclear Words* | | | | | | | | | | | | | |
| *Unclear This/That* | | | | | | | | | | | | | |
| *Phrase Placement* | | | | | | | | | | | | | |

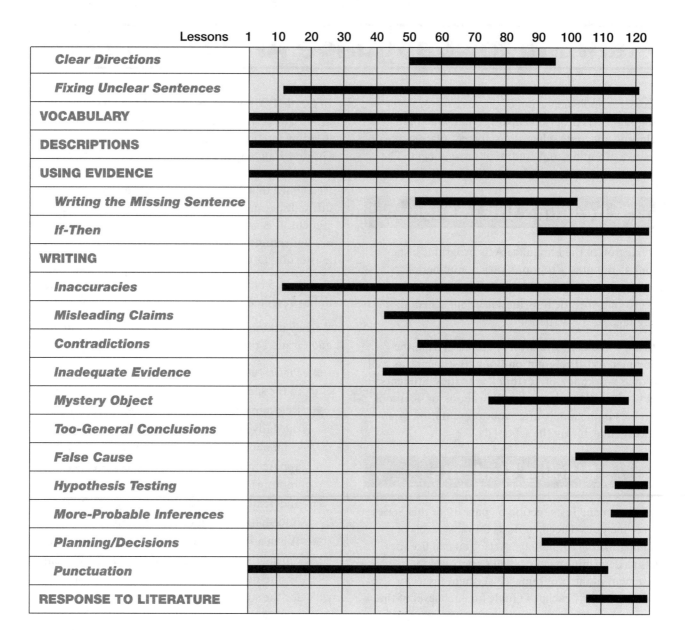

| Lessons | 1 | 10 | 20 | 30 | 40 | 50 | 60 | 70 | 80 | 90 | 100 | 110 | 120 |
|---|---|---|---|---|---|---|---|---|---|---|---|---|---|
| *Clear Directions* | | | | | | ▬ | ▬ | ▬ | ▬ | | | | |
| *Fixing Unclear Sentences* | | ▬ | ▬ | ▬ | ▬ | ▬ | ▬ | ▬ | ▬ | ▬ | ▬ | ▬ | |
| **VOCABULARY** | ▬ | ▬ | ▬ | ▬ | ▬ | ▬ | ▬ | ▬ | ▬ | ▬ | ▬ | ▬ | |
| **DESCRIPTIONS** | ▬ | ▬ | ▬ | ▬ | ▬ | ▬ | ▬ | ▬ | ▬ | ▬ | ▬ | ▬ | |
| **USING EVIDENCE** | ▬ | ▬ | ▬ | ▬ | ▬ | ▬ | ▬ | ▬ | ▬ | ▬ | ▬ | ▬ | |
| *Writing the Missing Sentence* | | | | | | ▬ | ▬ | ▬ | ▬ | | | | |
| *If-Then* | | | | | | | | | | ▬ | ▬ | ▬ | |
| **WRITING** | | | | | | | | | | | | | |
| *Inaccuracies* | | ▬ | ▬ | ▬ | ▬ | ▬ | ▬ | ▬ | ▬ | ▬ | ▬ | ▬ | |
| *Misleading Claims* | | | | | ▬ | ▬ | ▬ | ▬ | ▬ | ▬ | ▬ | ▬ | |
| *Contradictions* | | | | | | ▬ | ▬ | ▬ | ▬ | ▬ | ▬ | ▬ | |
| *Inadequate Evidence* | | | | | ▬ | ▬ | ▬ | ▬ | ▬ | ▬ | ▬ | ▬ | |
| *Mystery Object* | | | | | | | | ▬ | ▬ | ▬ | ▬ | | |
| *Too-General Conclusions* | | | | | | | | | | | | ▬ | |
| *False Cause* | | | | | | | | | | | ▬ | ▬ | |
| *Hypothesis Testing* | | | | | | | | | | | | ▬ | |
| *More-Probable Inferences* | | | | | | | | | | | | ▬ | |
| *Planning/Decisions* | | | | | | | | | | ▬ | ▬ | ▬ | |
| *Punctuation* | ▬ | ▬ | ▬ | ▬ | ▬ | ▬ | ▬ | ▬ | ▬ | ▬ | ▬ | | |
| **RESPONSE TO LITERATURE** | | | | | | | | | | | | ▬ | ▬ |

# Planning for Language Arts Instruction

Successful implementation of the *Reading Mastery* Language Arts programs involves many factors, including adequate scheduling, correct placement, effective grouping, and continuous assessment. The following sections examine these factors in detail.

## Scheduling the Lessons

Each lesson in the Language Arts programs lasts about 45 minutes. Programs vary in number of lessons. Consult the Teacher's Guide for a particular level to find specific information about scheduling Language Arts instruction.

During the lesson, you present exercises from the Language Arts Presentation Book to students, as well as some Workbook or Textbook activities. Students can work on the independent Workbook or Textbook activities immediately after your presentation or at another time during the school day.

## Placing Students

The Placement Tests section on page 30 of this Series Guide includes placement tests for most levels of *Reading Mastery* Language Arts. You can use the tests to determine each student's appropriate placement in the programs. (Placement tests can also be found in the Teacher's Guide for each level of the program.)

## Forming Groups

Student grouping in a typical classroom of 25 or more students depends on the program level. In the Grade K Language program, three groups are recommended: a large group (10–12) for the highest-performing students; a medium-sized group (8–10) for students in the middle; and a small group (no more than six) for the lowest-performing students. An alternative is to form two groups: one for the lowest-performing students and another for everybody else.

In Grade 1, if possible, students should be in smaller groups; ideally, the same groups they are in for the Reading strand. If such grouping is not possible, teach Grade 1 Language Arts to the entire class and try to find time to give the low performers extra practice. Recognize that teaching to the entire class is more difficult because it is harder for you to observe each student. It is important to make sure all your students are understanding the language concepts and mastering statement-production tasks.

Grades 2–5 of the Language Arts strand are designed to be presented to the entire class.

When working with smaller groups in the Grade K and Grade 1 programs, follow these guidelines:

- Place students with similar placement test scores in the same group.
- Regroup students based on their performance in the daily lessons. Students should be moved from one group to another when it becomes apparent that their placement is no longer appropriate. Students' responses to Workbook and Textbook exercises provide you with daily information about their performance.
- When a student transfers into your classroom during the school year, administer the Placement Test to determine which group is most suitable for the student. Thereafter, observe the student closely to ensure that the placement is appropriate. Students transferring into the program later in the year are often difficult to place. Some may require individual help before entering a group.
- Students who are absent a great deal should be treated like students who transfer late in the year.

## Program Assessments

Grades K and 2–5 of *Reading Mastery* Language Arts include criterion-referenced program assessments that can be used to measure student achievement within the program. The assessments are administered after every 10th lesson, except for Grade 5, where they are administered after every 20th lesson. Each assessment measures student understanding of a specific set of concepts from the exercises presented in the preceding 10 or 20 lessons.

Assessments in Grade K are oral tests that you present to each student individually. Assessments in Grades 2–5 are written tests that you administer to the group. The written tests appear in the student Workbook or Textbook, and administration instructions appear in the Language Arts Presentation Books. Students who do not do well on the assessments receive remedial exercises, which are specified in the program.

# Language Arts Placement Tests

This section includes placement tests for Grades K–1 and 3–5 of *Reading Mastery* Language Arts. (There is no placement test for Grade 2 Language Arts. Grade 2 is appropriate for students who have completed Grade 1 Language Arts and for students who are placed in the Grade 2 Reading strand.)

You can use the placement tests to determine which students are appropriately placed in which program, and where they should begin. (Placement tests can also be found in the Teacher's Guides.)

The contents of this section are listed in the next column. The section includes a Transition Lesson to be used with students who begin Grade K Language after Lesson 1.

| Test/Lesson | Page |
|---|---|
| Grade K Placement Test | 31 |
| Grade K Transition Lesson | 36 |
| Grade 1 Placement Test | 42 |
| Grade 3 Placement Test | 45 |
| Grade 4 Placement Test | 48 |
| Grade 5 Placement Test | 51 |

# Grade K Language Placement Test

The Placement Test that begins on the next page is to be administered individually to each child before language instruction begins. All testing should be completed during the first week of school.

## Before Giving the Test

The testing material consists of the Placement Test, the Picture Book, and the Placement Test Scoring Sheet. You will need a scoring sheet for each child in your class. (See page 35 for a scoring sheet that you can duplicate for each child.)

Familiarize yourself with the instructions, the Picture Book, and the scoring sheet before testing. Practice presenting the test items using these materials.

The test is divided into three parts. A child's score is based on the number of errors he or she makes.

- If a child makes more than three errors in Part 1, do not use Parts 2 or 3.
- If a child makes three or fewer errors in Part 1, continue testing the child in Part 2.
- If a child makes more than two errors in Part 2, stop testing; do not use Part 3.
- If a child makes two or fewer errors in Part 2, continue testing, and present all of the items in Part 3.

## How to Give the Test

1. Allow three to five minutes per child for administering the placement test.
2. Sit at a low table with the child, preferably in a quiet corner of the room.
3. Score the child's response on his or her scoring sheet as you present the test. Circle 0 to indicate a correct response to a test item. Circle 1 to indicate an incorrect response.
4. Accept all reasonable answers, using the suggested answers as guidelines.
5. On statement repetition items (9 and 11 in Part 1, for example), circle a 1 each time you have to repeat the statement until the student produces a correct response. Repeat the statement no more than four times. (If the student repeats the statement the first time you say it, circle the zero.)
6. At the end of Part I, total the 1s you have circled. Write the number of incorrect responses in the box.
7. Use the directions at the end of each part of the scoring sheet to determine if the student should be tested on the next part or if you should terminate the testing.
8. For administering Part 2, item 15, you will need a pencil with an eraser. For Part 3, items 1 through 4, you will need a big empty glass and a small glass full of water. For items 6 through 8 you will need a pencil.
9. When referring to the pictures in Parts 1 and 2, you may point to the pictures in the Picture Book or use the pictures in the test.

## Determining the Starting Lesson

The directions at the bottom of the scoring sheet indicate the lesson at which each child should be placed in the program.

- Children who score six or more errors in Part 1 begin at lesson 1.
- Children who score four or five errors in Part 1 begin at Lesson 11.
- Children who score six or more errors in Part 2 begin at Lesson 21.
- Children who score between three and five errors in Part 2 and children who score eight or more errors in Part 3 begin at lesson 31. Start these children in the fast cycle of the program.
- Children who score seven or fewer errors in Part 3 begin at lesson 41 and go into the fast-cycle program.

## Teaching the Transition Lesson

All children who do not begin the program with lesson 1 must be taught the transition lesson on the first day of language instruction. You will find the transition lesson on page 36 of this guide.

> **PLACEMENT TEST**

**Part 1**

(You may use the Picture Book, or use the pictures in the test, for items 8 through 13.)

1. Show me your nose.
   (The child must point to his/her nose.)
2. Show me your head.
   (The child may point anywhere on his/her head.)
3. Show me your ear.
   (The child may point to one or both ears.)
4. Show me your hand.
   (The child may hold up one hand or both hands.)
5. Show me your chin.
   (The child must point to his/her chin.)
6. Show me your cheek.
   (The child may touch one cheek or both cheeks.)
7. Show me your shoulder.
   (The child may point to one shoulder or both shoulders.)

8. (Point to the man.)
   What is this man doing?
   (Accept *Sleeping, Going to sleep,* or *Lying down.* Don't accept *Sleep, Eyes shut,* or *Got to sleep.*)
9. My turn to say the whole thing.
   **This man is sleeping.** Say that.
   *This* (or that) *man is sleeping.*

10. (Point to the girl.)
    What is this girl doing?
    (Accept *Eating, Eating a cookie,* or an entire correct sentence. Don't accept *Eat* or *Eat a cookie.*)
11. My turn to say the whole thing.
    **This girl is eating.** Say that.
    *This girl is eating* or
    *This girl is eating a cookie.*

12. (Point to the cat.)
    What is this cat doing?
    (Accept *Climbing the tree, Going up the tree, Climbing on a tree, Climbing up there,* or *Climbing.*)
13. My turn to say the whole thing.
    **This cat is climbing the tree.** Say that.
    *This cat is climbing the tree.*
14. What's your whole name?
    (The child must give first and last name; middle name is optional.)
15. What's your first name?
    (The child must give first name only.)

**End of Part 1**

## Part 2

You may use the Picture Book (or use the pictures in the test) for items 1 through 7 and item 14. You will need a pencil with an eraser and a point for item 15.

1. (Point to the picture of the car.)
   Tell me what is **in front of** the car.
   (Accept *Ball* or *A ball.*)
2. Tell me what is **on** the car.
   *A dog.*
3. Tell me what is **in** the car.
   (Accept *A man* or *A boy.*)
4. Look at the dog. Is the dog sleeping?
   *No.*
5. My turn to say the whole thing.
   **This dog is not sleeping.** Say that.
   *This dog is not sleeping.*
6. Look at the dog. Is the dog climbing a tree?
   (Accept *No* or *No, he's on the car.*)
7. My turn to say the whole thing.
   **This dog is not climbing a tree.** Say that.
   *This dog is not climbing a tree.*
8. Show me your chest.
   (The child is to point to his/her chest.)
9. Show me your waist.
   (The child is to point to his/her waist.)
10. Put your hand on your head, and hold it there.
    Look at me. (Touch your own nose.)
    What am I doing?
    (Accept *Touching your nose* or *Putting your hand on your nose.*)
    Keep your hand on your head.

11. (The child should still be touching his/her head.)
    What are you doing?
    (Accept *Touching my head, Putting my hand on my head,* or an entire correct sentence.)
12. (The child must answer both parts correctly to score 0.)
    Hold your hand **over** your leg.
    (The child must hold his/her hand over leg.)
    Tell me where you are holding your hand.
    *Over my leg.*
13. (The child must answer both parts correctly to score 0.)
    Hold your hand **under** your leg.
    (The child must hold his/her hand under his/her leg.)
    Tell me where you are holding your hand.
    *Under my leg.*

14. (Point to the apple.)
    This is **an** apple. What is this?
    (Accept *An apple.* Don't accept *Apple* or *A apple.*)
15. (The child must answer all three parts correctly to score 0. Stop testing if the child misses one item.)
    a. (Point to the eraser of a pencil.)
       What's this part of a pencil called?
       (Accept *Eraser* or *An (the) eraser.*)
    b. (Point to the pencil point.)
       What is this part of a pencil called?
       (Accept *Point, A point,* or *Lead.*
       Don't accept *Drawer* or *Writer.*)
    c. (Point to the whole pencil.)
       What do you call the whole thing?
       (Accept *Pencil* or *A pencil.*)

## End of Part 2

## Part 3

(You will need a big glass that is empty and a small glass that is full for items 1 through 4. You will need a pencil for items 6 through 8.)

(Present a big glass and a small glass. The big glass should be empty, and the small glass full.)

1. Touch the **big** glass.

   (The child touches the big glass.) Put your hand down.

2. Touch the glass that is **empty.**

   (The child touches the empty glass.) Put your hand down.

3. Touch the glass that is **full.**

   (The child touches the full glass.) Put your hand down.

4. Touch the **small** glass.

   (The child touches the small glass.) Put your hand down.

5. My turn to say the days of the week: Sunday, Monday, Tuesday, Wednesday, Thursday, Friday, Saturday.

   (Do not repeat the days more than twice.)

   Say the days of the week. Start with Sunday.

   *Sunday, Monday, Tuesday, Wednesday, Thursday, Friday, Saturday.*

6. (The child must answer all three parts correctly to score 0.)

   (You place the pencil on the table.)

   Is the pencil **on** the table? *Yes.*

   (Hold the pencil over the table.)

   Is the pencil **on** the table? *No.*

   (Keep holding the pencil over the table.)

   **Was** the pencil on the table? *Yes.*

7. (Keep holding the pencil.)

   My turn to say the whole thing.

   The pencil was on the table. Say that.

   *The pencil was on the table.*

8. Where **is** the pencil?

   (Accept *In your hand, Over the table,* or *Off the table.*)

9. (The child must answer all four parts correctly to score 0.)

   Touch your ears.

   (The child must touch both ears.)

   Touch your leg.

   (The child must touch one leg.)

   Touch your ear.

   (The child must touch one ear.)

   Touch your legs.

   (The child must touch both legs.)

10. Put your hand in back of your head. (The child may put one or both hands in back of his/her head or neck.) Put your hand down.

11. Point to the floor, and point to the ceiling.

    (The child must point to the floor **and** to the ceiling.)

12. What do we call the white fluffy things in the sky? *Clouds.*

13. What do we call a person who fixes teeth?

    (Accept *A dentist* or *A doctor.*)

14. Name three kinds of food.

    (Accept all appropriate responses.)

15. Name three kinds of vehicles.

    (Accept all appropriate responses.)

## End of Test

**Grade K Language**

# PLACEMENT TEST SCORING SHEET

**Student's Name** _____ **Date** _____

| PART 1 | | | PART 2 | | | PART 3 | | |
|---|---|---|---|---|---|---|---|---|
| Items | Correct Responses | Incorrect Responses | Items | Correct Responses | Incorrect Responses | Items | Correct Responses | Incorrect Responses |
| 1 | 0 | 1 | 1 | 0 | 1 | 1 | 0 | 1 |
| 2 | 0 | 1 | 2 | 0 | 1 | 2 | 0 | 1 |
| 3 | 0 | 1 | 3 | 0 | 1 | 3 | 0 | 1 |
| 4 | 0 | 1 | 4 | 0 | 1 | 4 | 0 | 1 |
| 5 | 0 | 1 | 5 | 0 | 1 1 1 1 | 5 | 0 | 1 1 |
| 6 | 0 | 1 | 6 | 0 | 1 | 6 | 0 | 1 |
| 7 | 0 | 1 | 7 | 0 | 1 1 1 1 | 7 | 0 | 1 1 1 1 |
| 8 | 0 | 1 | 8 | 0 | 1 | 8 | 0 | 1 |
| 9 | 0 | 1 1 1 1 | 9 | 0 | 1 | 9 | 0 | 1 |
| 10 | 0 | 1 | 10 | 0 | 1 | 10 | 0 | 1 |
| 11 | 0 | 1 1 1 1 | 11 | 0 | 1 | 11 | 0 | 1 |
| 12 | 0 | 1 | 12 | 0 | 1 | 12 | 0 | 1 |
| 13 | 0 | 1 1 1 1 | 13 | 0 | 1 | 13 | 0 | 1 |
| 14 | 0 | 1 | 14 | 0 | 1 | 14 | 0 | 1 |
| 15 | 0 | 1 | 15 | 0 | 1 | 15 | 0 | 1 |
| Total of All Incorrect Responses | | [ ] | Total of All Incorrect Responses | | [ ] | Total of All Incorrect Responses | | [ ] |
| | | Score | | | Score | | | Score |

| Student's Score | Starts at Lesson | Student's Score | Starts at Lesson | Student's Score | Starts at Lesson |
|---|---|---|---|---|---|
| 6 or more | 1 | 6 or more | 21 | 8 or more | 31 |
| 4 or 5 | 11 | 3 to 5 | 31 | 0 to 7 | 41 |
| | (Circle the lesson) | | (Circle the lesson) | | (Circle the lesson) |
| 0 to 3 | Continue testing in part 2. | 0 to 2 | Continue testing in part 3. | | |
| | (Check box) [ ] | | (Check box) [ ] | | |

## Grade K Language Transition Lesson

The Transition Lesson is intended to help students who place at lesson 11, 21, 31, or 41 learn how to participate in a Grade K Language lesson. The Transition Lesson contains exercises drawn from the first 17 lessons of the program. The lesson is to be taught to all groups that begin the program with lesson 11, 21, 31, or 41. It is not to be used with groups that start at lesson 1.

The Transition Lesson should be presented on the first day of instruction. By the end of the lesson, students will learn that

- the point-and-touch signal and the hand-drop signal indicate when they are to respond.
- the instruction Say the whole thing indicates that they are to make a complete statement.
- a complete statement is not called for unless you say, Say the whole thing.

On the second day of instruction, teach the lesson at which the group is to begin: for example, lesson 21, if that is where the group placed. Students who are placed at lesson 21, 31, or 41 may have some difficulty with the contents of the first few lessons. Make sure their responses are firm on all the exercises even if you need two periods to present a lesson.

**The Transition Lesson**

The transition lesson is for children who place beyond lesson 1.

**EXERCISE 1  Actions—Following Directions and Body Parts**

1. Get ready to do some actions. Watch my hand. Remember to wait for the signal.
  a. Everybody, stand up. (Signal. Children are to stand up.)
  b. Everybody, touch your nose. (Signal. Wait.)
  c. Everybody, sit down. (Signal. Wait.)
  d. Everybody, touch your hand. (Signal. Wait.)
  e. Everybody, put your hand down. (Signal.)
  f. (Repeat steps a through e until all children respond to your signal.)

2. Now let's talk more about those actions.
  a. Everybody, stand up. (Signal.) What are you doing? (Signal.) *Standing up.*
  b. Everybody, touch your nose. (Signal.) What are you doing? (Signal.) *Touching my nose.* ●
  c. Everybody, sit down. (Signal.) What are you doing? (Signal.) *Sitting down.*
  d. Everybody, touch your hand. (Signal.) What are you doing? (Signal.) *Touching my hand.* Everybody, put your hand down. (Signal.)

3. Let's do that again.
  (Repeat part 2 until all children can perform the actions and say what they are doing.)

**EXERCISE 2  Identity Statements**

1. We're going to talk about a girl.
  a. (Ask a girl in the group to stand up.) Everybody, what is this? (Signal.) *A girl.* Yes, a girl.
  b. My turn. I can say the whole thing. This is a girl. Listen again. This is a girl.
  c. Say the whole thing with me. (Signal. Respond with children.) *This is a girl.*
  d. Again. (Signal. Respond with children.) *This is a girl.*
  e. (Repeat step d until all children are making the statement with you.)
  f. Your turn. All by yourselves. Say the whole thing. (Signal. Do not respond with children.) *This is a girl.*
  g. (Repeat step f until all children can make the statement.)

2. We're going to talk about a boy.
  a. (Ask a boy in the group to stand up.) Everybody, what is this? (Signal.) *A boy.* Yes, a boy.
  b. My turn. I can say the whole thing. This is a boy. Listen again. This is a boy.
  c. Say the whole thing with me. (Signal. Respond with children.) *This is a boy.*
  d. Again. (Signal. Respond with children.) *This is a boy.*
  e. (Repeat step d until all children are making the statement with you.)
  f. Now it's your turn. All by yourselves. Say the whole thing. (Signal. Do not respond with children.) *This is a boy.*
  g. (Repeat step f until all children can make the statement.)

**Individual Turns**

(Call on different children to make the statements.)

---

## CORRECTIONS

**EXERCISE 1**

● **Error**
(Children don't say *Touching my nose.*)

**Correction**

1. Touching my nose. Say it with me. (Signal. Respond with children.) *Touching my nose.*

2. Again. (Signal. Respond with children.) *Touching my nose.*

3. All by yourselves. Say it. (Signal. Do not respond with children.) *Touching my nose.*

4. (Have children put their hands down.)

5. (Repeat part 2b.)

In this exercise, children learn to identify objects and to follow the point and touch signals.

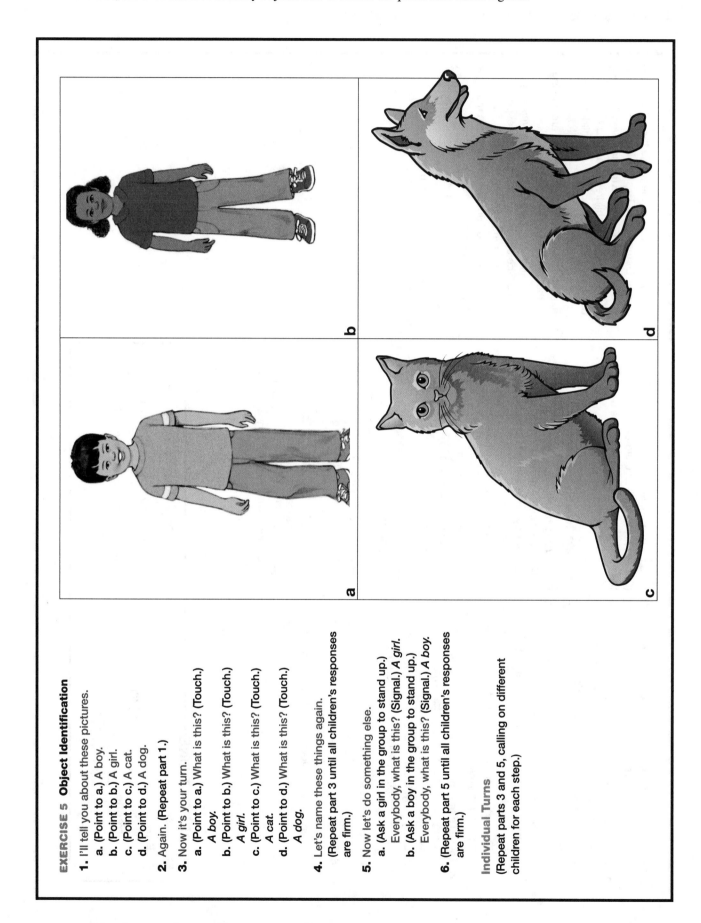

EXERCISE 5  Object Identification

1. I'll tell you about these pictures.
    a. (Point to a.) A boy.
    b. (Point to b.) A girl.
    c. (Point to c.) A cat.
    d. (Point to d.) A dog.

2. Again. (Repeat part 1.)

3. Now it's your turn.
    a. (Point to a.) What is this? (Touch.)
       *A boy.*
    b. (Point to b.) What is this? (Touch.)
       *A girl.*
    c. (Point to c.) What is this? (Touch.)
       *A cat.*
    d. (Point to d.) What is this? (Touch.)
       *A dog.*

4. Let's name these things again.
    (Repeat part 3 until all children's responses
    are firm.)

5. Now let's do something else.
    a. (Ask a girl in the group to stand up.)
       Everybody, what is this? (Signal.) *A girl.*
    b. (Ask a boy in the group to stand up.)
       Everybody, what is this? (Signal.) *A boy.*

6. (Repeat part 5 until all children's responses
    are firm.)

Individual Turns
(Repeat parts 3 and 5, calling on different
children for each step.)

In this exercise, you introduce the children to the complete statement.

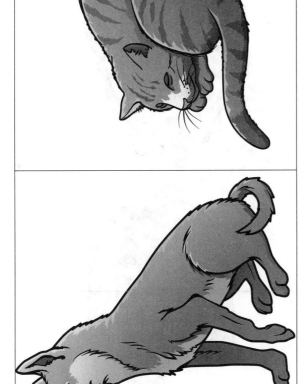

**EXERCISE 7  Identity Statements**

1. We're going to talk about a dog. When I touch it, you tell me about it.
   a. (Point to the dog.) Everybody, what is this? (Touch.) *A dog.*
      Yes, a dog.
   b. My turn. I can say the whole thing. This is a dog. Listen again. This is a dog. Say the whole thing with me. (Touch. Respond with children.) *This is a dog.*
   c. Again. (Touch. Respond with children.) *This is a dog.*
      (Repeat until all children can make the statement with you.)
   d. Your turn. All by yourselves. Say the whole thing. (Touch. Do not respond with children.) *This is a dog.*
      Again. (Touch. Do not respond with children.) *This is a dog.*

2. (Repeat part 1 until all children can make the statement.)

3. We're going to talk about a cat. When I touch it, you tell me about it.
   a. (Point to the cat.) Everybody, what is this? (Touch.) *A cat.*
      Yes, a cat.
   b. My turn. I can say the whole thing. This is a cat. Listen again. This is a cat. Say the whole thing with me. (Touch. Respond with children.) *This is a cat.*
   c. Again. (Touch. Respond with children.) *This is a cat.*
      (Repeat until all children are making the statement with you.)
   d. Your turn. All by yourselves. Say the whole thing. (Touch. Do not respond with children.) *This is a cat.*
   e. Again. (Touch. Do not respond with children.) *This is a cat.*

4. (Repeat part 3 until all children can make the statement.)

**Individual Turns**
(Call on different children to say the whole thing about each picture.)

In this exercise, the children identify objects and make complete statements in response to your instructions.

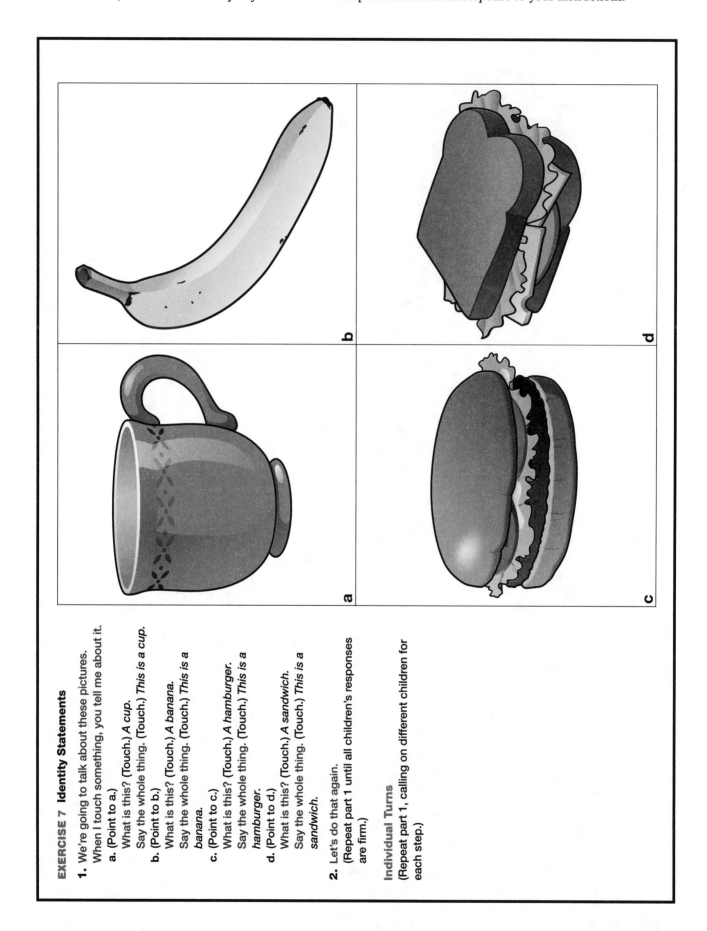

**EXERCISE 7 Identity Statements**

**1.** We're going to talk about these pictures.
When I touch something, you tell me about it.

**a.** (Point to a.)
What is this? (Touch.) *A cup.*
Say the whole thing. (Touch.) *This is a cup.*

**b.** (Point to b.)
What is this? (Touch.) *A banana.*
Say the whole thing. (Touch.) *This is a banana.*

**c.** (Point to c.)
What is this? (Touch.) *A hamburger.*
Say the whole thing. (Touch.) *This is a hamburger.*

**d.** (Point to d.)
What is this? (Touch.) *A sandwich.*
Say the whole thing. (Touch.) *This is a sandwich.*

**2.** Let's do that again.
(Repeat part 1 until all children's responses are firm.)

**Individual Turns**
(Repeat part 1, calling on different children for each step.)

In this exercise, the children learn to make an action statement about a picture.

**EXERCISE 5  Action Statements—Pictures**

**1.** We're going to talk about some actions.
   **a.** (Point to the girl.) Everybody, what is this? (Touch.) *A girl.*
   Say the whole thing. (Touch.) *This is a girl.*
   **b.** Listen. What is this girl doing? (Touch.) *Standing.*
   **c.** Let's say the whole thing about what this girl is doing. (Touch. Respond with children.) *This girl is standing.*
   **d.** Again. (Touch.) *This girl is standing.*
   **e.** All by yourselves. Say the whole thing about what this girl is doing. (Touch.) *This girl is standing.*
   **f.** (Repeat steps a through e until all children's responses are firm.)

**2.** Now we'll talk about some more actions.
   **a.** (Point to the dog.) Everybody, what is this? (Touch.) *A dog.*
   Say the whole thing. (Touch.) *This is a dog.*
   **b.** What is this dog doing? (Touch.) *Sitting.*
   **c.** Say the whole thing about what this dog is doing. (Touch. Do not respond with children.) *This dog is sitting.*
   **d.** Again. (Touch.) *This dog is sitting.*
   **e.** (Repeat steps a through d until all children's responses are firm.)

**3.** Get ready to do some more.
   **a.** (Point to the cat.) Everybody, what is this? (Touch.) *A cat.*
   Say the whole thing. (Touch.) *This is a cat.*
   **b.** What is the cat doing? (Touch.) *Standing.*
   **c.** Say the whole thing about what this cat is doing. (Touch.) *This cat is standing.*
   **d.** Again. (Touch.) *This cat is standing.*
   **e.** (Repeat steps a through d until all children's responses are firm.)

**4.** Let's do those again.
   **a.** (Point to the girl.) Everybody, what is this? (Touch.) *A girl.*
   **b.** What is this girl doing? (Touch.) *Standing.*
   **c.** Say the whole thing about what this girl is doing. (Touch.) *This girl is standing.*

**5.** (Repeat parts 2 and 3 until all children's responses are firm.)

**Individual Turns**
(Repeat the exercise, calling on different children for each step.)

**End of Transition Lesson**

## Grade 1 Language Arts Placement Test

The Grade 1 Language Arts component is appropriate for all students who have completed Grade K Language. Use the Grade 1 Placement Test to determine whether students who have not completed Grade K have the skills needed to place in Grade 1. Students who make five or fewer errors on the test have the necessary skills.

### How to Administer the Test

1. Plan to administer the Placement Test individually to each child who has not been taught *Reading Mastery* Grade K Language. Allow three to five minutes for each child you will test.

2. Make a copy of the score sheet on page 44 for each child.

3. Familiarize yourself with the instructions and the score sheet before testing.

4. Sit at the same side of a low table with the child, preferably in a quiet corner of the room.

5. Score the child's response on the score sheet as you present each test item. Circle 0 to indicate a correct response to a test item and 1 to indicate an incorrect response. Each error counts as 1, and the child's score is the total number of errors he or she makes.

6. Stop testing as soon as a child makes six errors. If possible, give the test for Grade K Language. If a child makes five or fewer errors, he or she can begin instruction in Grade 1 Language Arts.

### Part 1

(Place a sheet of paper on the table. Hand the child a penny. If the child answers "there" in any of the following tasks, say Tell me **where** it is.)

1. Put the penny on the piece of paper. (Wait.)
- Tell me. **Where** is the penny? (The child is to put the penny on the paper and *say On the paper.*)
2. Now hold the penny over the piece of paper. (Wait.)
- Tell me. **Where** is the penny now? (The child is to hold the penny so that it is over the piece of paper, but not touching, and *say Over the paper.*)
3. Now put the penny next to the piece of paper. (Wait.)
- Tell me. **Where** is the penny now? (The child is to put the penny next to the paper and *say Next to the paper.*)
4. Put the penny under the piece of paper. (Wait.)
- Tell me. **Where** is the penny now? (The child is to put the penny under the paper and *say Under the paper.*)

### Part 2

I'll say sentences. Say them just the way I say them.

5. Listen. (Pause.) If it rains, the cows will get wet. Say that. (Repeat the statement once if the child fails on the first attempt. If the child repeats the statement correctly on either the first or second trial, score the item as correct.)
6. Listen. (Pause.) They were having a good time on their vacation. Say that. (Repeat the statement once if the child fails on the first attempt. If the child repeats the statement correctly on the first or second trial, score the item as correct.)

## Part 3

Look at the picture.

7. Two of these elephants are **wearing** the same thing.
- Point to the two elephants that are **wearing** the same thing.
(The child is to point to elephant 1 and elephant 3.)
8. What are they wearing that is the same?
(The child is to respond *hats* or *a hat*.)
9. Two of these elephants are **holding** the same thing.
- Point to the two elephants that are **holding** the same thing.
(The child is to point to elephant 1 and elephant 2.)
10. What are they holding that is the same?
(The child is to respond *flowers* or *a flower.*)

## Part 4

Tell me if I hold up some of my fingers, all of my fingers, or none of my fingers.

(If the child identifies the number of fingers in any of the following tasks, ask: Am I holding up some of my fingers, all of my fingers, or none of my fingers?)

11. (Hold up all ten fingers.) What am I holding up? (The child is to respond *all of your fingers* or *all.*)
12. (Hold up seven fingers.) What am I holding up? (The child is to respond *some of your fingers* or *some.*)
13. (Hold up three fingers.) What am I holding up? (The child is to respond *some of your fingers* or *some.*)
14. (Hold up a closed fist.) What am I holding up? (The child is to respond *none of your fingers* or *none.*)

## Part 5

I'm going to tell you a story about a tiger. I'm going to tell the story one time, so listen carefully. Here is the story.

- The tiger lived in the jungle. The tiger hunted at night. The tiger did not hunt during the day. It slept all day long.

(Accept all reasonable responses to the following items.)

15. Who hunted? *The tiger.*
16. Where did the tiger live? *In the jungle.*
17. When did the tiger hunt? *At night.*
18. When did the tiger sleep? *In the day.*
19. What did the tiger do during the day? *Slept* (or) *Sleeping.*
20. What did the tiger do during the night? *Hunted* (or) *Hunt.*

**Student's name** _____

**Date** _____

| Items | Correct Responses | Incorrect Responses |
|-------|-------------------|---------------------|
| **PART 1** | | |
| 1 | 0 | 1 |
| 2 | 0 | 1 |
| 3 | 0 | 1 |
| 4 | 0 | 1 |
| **PART 2** | | |
| 5 | 0 | 1 |
| 6 | 0 | 1 |
| **PART 3** | | |
| 7 | 0 | 1 |
| 8 | 0 | 1 |
| 9 | 0 | 1 |
| 10 | 0 | 1 |
| **PART 4** | | |
| 11 | 0 | 1 |
| 12 | 0 | 1 |
| 13 | 0 | 1 |
| 14 | 0 | 1 |
| **PART 5** | | |
| 15 | 0 | 1 |
| 16 | 0 | 1 |
| 17 | 0 | 1 |
| 18 | 0 | 1 |
| 19 | 0 | 1 |
| 20 | 0 | 1 |

**Total Score** _____

## Grade 3 Language Arts Placement Test

Grade 3 Language Arts is appropriate for students who read on at least a beginning third-grade level, who can copy words at no less than 10 words per minute, and who can follow basic directions. Students who do not meet these criteria will have trouble performing many of the activities presented in Grade 3 Language Arts.

The Grade 3 Language Arts Placement Test evaluates students' performance at following directions and copying a passage. A blackline master of the test appears on page 46.

### Administering the Test

The test is administered to the group and requires about 10 minutes for students to complete. Use the script below to present the test.

1. (Give each student a copy of the test. Students are to write their name in the space on the top.)
2. (Note: The following are non-scorable warm-up items.)
- Get ready to follow some directions.
- Touch the picture of the dog.
   (Observe students and give feedback.)
- The dog is not the first or second or third picture. Raise your hand when you know the number for the dog.
- Everybody, what's the number for the dog? (Signal.) *6.*

3. (Note: The following are scorable items. Allow 5 seconds for each item.)
- I'll tell you directions. Do exactly what the directions tell you to do. Get your pencils ready.
- Listen: Circle the first picture.
   (Pause 5 seconds.)
- New directions: Make a box around the last picture.
   (Pause 5 seconds.)
- New directions: Make a line **under** the picture that is just after the bird.
- Listen again: Make a line **under** the picture that is just after the bird.
   (Pause 5 seconds).
- New directions: Make a line **over** the picture that is just before the snake.
- Listen again: Make a line **over** the picture that is just before the snake.
   (Pause 5 seconds.)
- Everybody, put your pencil down and don't touch it until I tell you.
4. Touch the little story that is in the box.
- I'll read that story. Follow along: **Three men sat in their boat. One of those men jumped into the water. A big fish chased him.**
- Everybody, touch the lines below the story. You're going to copy that whole story.
- Everybody, touch the letter A. You'll start right after the letter A. You'll copy the story just the way it is written. You'll spell all the words correctly. You'll put in the capital letters and the periods just the way they are shown in the story.
- The first sentence of the story is: **Three men sat in their boat.** That's the first sentence you'll copy. Then you'll copy the rest of the story. Pencils ready. You have two minutes. Get ready. Go.
- (Time students. After 2 minutes, say) Everybody, if you're not finished, stop now and put your pencil down.
- (Collect tests.)

Name: _____     Date: _____

Three men sat in their boat. One of those men jumped into the water. A big fish chased him.

A.

| | | | | | |
|---|---|---|---|---|---|
| 1. Number of errors on picture items | 0 | **1** | 2 | 3 | 4 | |
| 2. Number of omitted words (words not copied) | 0 | 1 | **2** | 3 | 4 | 5 | ☐ |
| 3. Number of copied words misspelled | 0 | 1 | **2** | 3 | 4 | 5 | ☐ |

## Scoring the Test

On each student's test form, record the number of errors.

Line 1: Circle the number of errors the student made on **picture items.** If the child missed no items, circle 0. If the child missed all 4 picture items, circle 4. An answer key for the pictures appears below:

Line 2: Circle the number of **omitted words** (words not copied). Read each student's story. Make sure all the sentences have the correct words. Mark any places where the student omitted words. Count the number of omitted words (those overlooked or those at the end of the story that were not written). If the number is 5 or less, circle the appropriate number on line 2. If the number is more than 5, write the number in the box at the end of line 2.

Line 3: Circle the number of **misspelled words.** Mark each misspelled word. Count the number. If the number is 5 or less, circle the appropriate number on line 3. If the number is more than 5, write the number in the box at the end of line 3.

## Placement Criteria

Students should not be placed in Grade 3 Language Arts unless they meet the criteria described below.

1.  **The student should read on at least the beginning third-grade level.** If you have doubts about the student's reading ability, direct the student to read the following sentences from part A of Lesson 1:

| | | |
|---|---|---|
| 1. The three men were brothers. | reports | does not report |
| 2. Three men fished from a boat. | reports | does not report |
| 4. A big dog stood in the boat. | reports | does not report |
| 5. All the men wore hats. | reports | does not report |
| 8. A large fish was on the end of the line. | reports | does not report |

Point to each item the student is to read and say Read this sentence. If the student gets stuck on a word, tell the word after about 3 seconds. The student should complete the reading in no more than 45 seconds and should make no more than 3 decoding errors. Students who exceed these limits probably do not read well enough to benefit from Grade 3 Language Arts.

2.  **The student should pass all the criteria listed on lines 1, 2, and 3 at the bottom of the Placement Test.** The criterion for each line is indicated by the boldfaced number.

| | |
|---|---|
| 1. Number of errors on picture items | 0 **1** 2 3 4 |
| 2. Number of omitted words (words not copied) | 0 1 **2** 3 4 5 |
| 3. Number of copied words misspelled | 0 1 **2** 3 4 5 |

If the student's number is to the right of the boldfaced number, the student fails that criterion. If the student makes more than one error on the picture items, the student fails. If the student makes more than two errors on omitted or copied words, the student fails.

If a student passes all the criteria but one and just barely misses meeting that criterion, the student could be placed in Grade 3 Language Arts.

## Grade 4 Language Arts Placement Test

Grade 4 Language Arts is appropriate for students who have mastered the basics of narrative writing and can write a coherent passage. Students who place in the Reading strand of *Reading Mastery Signature Edition,* Grade 4, will generally have sufficient writing skills. For those students, using the Grade 4 Language Arts Placement Test may not be necessary.

### Administering the Test

A blackline master of the Grade 4 Language Arts Placement Test appears on page 49. Each student will need a copy of the test, lined paper, and a pencil. Use the following script to administer the test.

1. Look at the pictures. You're going to write a story that tells what happened. You'll begin your story with the sentence in the first box. That sentence says: **Ray, Mario and Lisa stood on the deck of the boat.**

2. The first picture shows what happened at the beginning of the story. The second picture shows how the story ended. Lots of things must have happened between the first picture and the second picture.

3. I'll read the words in the vocabulary box below the pictures: **anchor, face mask, air tank, pressure, jewels, coins, diving equipment, dove, exclaimed, sharks.** Be sure to spell those words correctly if you use them in your passage.

4. I'll make up a beginning to the story:

    Ray, Mario and Lisa stood on the deck of the boat. They looked at a map. They were getting ready to search for a sunken treasure. Mario said, "I hope we find the treasure."

    Lisa said, "People say the treasure is worth a fortune." The divers put on their diving equipment and stood by the side of the boat.

5. Start with the sentence in the box that tells what Ray, Lisa and Mario did. Then write an interesting story. Tell what the characters did and what they said. Be sure to tell all the important things that must have happened between the pictures. You have 20 minutes.

6. (After 20 minutes, collect the students' papers.)

Name: _____ Date: _____

Write an interesting story. Use lined paper.

- Start with the sentence in the first box.
- Tell what the characters did and what they said.

Ray, Mario and Lisa stood on the deck of the boat.

Ray    Lisa

Mario

I hope we find the treasure.

People say the treasure is worth a fortune.

anchor       face mask       air tank       pressure       jewels

coins       diving equipment       dove       exclaimed       sharks

## Marking the Test

Establishing fair criteria for scoring a writing test is difficult, but gaining a sense of the range of students who should be placed in Grade 4 Language Arts is quite easy. If you wish, you can circle various writing problems in each student's test. When you find that your circles start to overlap, the student is probably too low for the program.

The examples below show the range of students who should be placed in Grade 4 Language Arts and those who are too low for the program. The passages are taken from actual student writing and are not made up for illustration purposes. Read the passages and notice the writing tendencies of the better students and those who are too low for the program. (To read more sample passages, consult the *Teacher's Guide* for Grade 4 Language Arts.)

The following sample is from a student who is prepared for Grade 4 Language Arts. The writing is coherent and clear. The student uses a variety of sentence types, and the punctuation is basically correct.

> *. . . They dove into the water and sunk into the deep until they disappeared. They had forgotten to put the anchor down in the water. Under the water everything looked pitch black so it was a good thing they remembered to bring flashlights. Also the pressure underneath the water was tougher and heavier. They separated themselves but not too much so they wouldn't get lost. Mario felt something on the floor and called Ray and Lisa to come help. They had found the treasure.*

The following sample is from a student who has an understanding of how to construct a narrative passage but has gaps in punctuation and clarity. This student can be placed in Grade 4 Language Arts but is likely to need support.

> *. . . Just then, Lisa shouted I found something. Mario, and Ray looked and looked to see what she found. Oh, look it's a crown Ray said. So they dug for more treasure. They found jewels, diamonds and coins. They kept digging until the next morning. So around 7:45 AM the next morning they found more things than they really needed. They gathered there dividing equipment and steered the boat all the way back to where they needed to go.*

The following example is from a student who does not have the basic writing skills needed for Grade 4 Language Arts. The passage has run-on sentences and sentence fragments, and it lacks verb agreement and tense consistency. This student needs systematic and explicit instruction in basic writing and would be more appropriately placed in Grade 3 Language Arts.

> *. . . When Ray was swiming with Mario. Ray hit his back on the treasure. So Lisa wint to Mario and Ray everybody carry the treasre up and then Lisa use a anchor to open the treasure. Then it dove open coins and diamonds, rubies pop open when they took out the jewels they seen necklaces and perls stook on the bottoms of the treasure*

## Grade 5 Language Arts Placement Test

Grade 5 Language Arts is appropriate for students who have completed Grade 4 Language Arts. The Grade 5 Placement Test can be used to determine whether students who have not completed Grade 4 have the skills needed for Grade 5.

### Administering the Test

A blackline master of the Grade 5 Language Arts Placement Test appears on page 52. Each student will need a copy of the test, lined paper, and a pencil. Use the following script to administer the test.

1. Find part 1. ✔
- Some of these items are sentences. Some are not. All the items begin with a capital letter and end with a period, but don't be fooled. Not all of them are sentences.
- Write the number of each item that is a sentence. Don't write the numbers for the items that are not sentences. Raise your hand when you're finished.
- (Observe students but do not give feedback.)

2. Part 2 shows a passage that is not written well. After each period is a number that tells how many mistakes are in the sentence.
- You're going to rewrite the passage so it has no mistakes. Write clear sentences. Don't change anything in the original passage unless it is a mistake. Raise your hand when you've written the passage so it has no mistakes.
- (Observe students but do not give feedback.)

3. Part 3 has two underlined sentences at the beginning of the passage. These sentences say **He finally decided to get it fixed. He took it there.** We don't know what **it** is, and we don't know where **there** is.
- Read the passage carefully. Find out what **it** refers to and what **there** refers to. Then rewrite the underlined sentences with words that tell what **it** is and the **place** he took it to. Raise your hand when you're finished.
- (Observe students but do not give feedback.)
- (Collect papers.)

## Grade 5 Placement Test Blackline Master

Name: _____ Date: _____

## PART 1

Each item begins with a capital and ends with a period, but some of the items are not sentences and should not be punctuated the way they are shown. Write the number of each item that is a sentence.

1. They talked.

2. Before school opened the other morning.

3. Under the stairs and running around the basement.

4. Timmy hit the baseball.

5. In the evening, the bugs came out.

6. Why Fred could not have gone to the meeting.

7. How I met my best friend.

8. Make a circle that is one inch across.

9. Sit down.

10. His statement indicated that he didn't see the accident.

## PART 2

Rewrite the passage. The number after each period tells the number of changes you must make.

Jan collected butterflies some was small and some was large. (5) She told her friends that she were going to catch a rare pink butterfly and she went out with a net and she came back with four butterflies. (5)

## PART 3

Rewrite the underlined sentences so they are clear.

He finally decided to get it fixed. He took it there. Bill asked the mechanic, "How much will it cost to get it fixed?"

The mechanic at Al's Garage looked at it for a long time. Finally, the mechanic said, "I'll have to charge over $500 to fix up this old car. I'm not sure it's worth fixing."

Bill loved his old car, but getting it fixed would cost too much money. Bill drove his old car away from Al's Garage.

## Answer Key

**Part 1**  1, 4, 5, 8, 9, 10

**Part 2**  (Possible changes are set in bold and enclosed in brackets. Accept other correct answers. Each sentence should have five changes.)

> Jan collected butterflies**[.] [S]**ome **[were]** small**[,]** and some **[were]** large.
> She told her friends that she **[was]** going to catch a rare pink butterfly**[.] [S]**he went out with a net**[.] [She]** came back with four butterflies.

**Part 3**

> He finally decided to get **an/his** [require either **an** or **his**] **old** [use of **old** is optional] car fixed. He took it to **a mechanic** or **Al's garage** or **a garage** [require use of one location].

## Scoring the Test

### Part 1

- Total possible points: 12
- Passing criterion: 8
- Score two points for every correct item; deduct two points for every non-sentence listed.

### Part 2

- Total possible points: 10
- Passing criterion: 7
- Deduct one point for every punctuation mark or capital letter that does not correspond to the key.

### Part 3

- Total possible points: 10
- Passing criterion: 9
- Deduct two points for each sentence that does not convey an adequate meaning.

## Placement Criteria

Students who fail more than one part of the test should not be placed in Grade 5 Language Arts. If more than one-third of the class fails more than one part of the test, the class should not be placed in Grade 5 Language Arts.

To determine appropriate placement for students who do not meet the placement criteria for Grade 5 Language Arts, administer the Placement Test for Grade 4 Language Arts.

# Sample Language Arts Lessons

This section contains one sample lesson from each grade of the Language Arts strand of *Reading Mastery Signature Edition*. Use the table below to locate the sample lesson for a particular grade.

| Grade | Sample Lesson | Page |
|-------|---------------|------|
| K | 75 | 54 |
| 1 | 12 | 79 |
| 2 | 35 | 87 |
| 3 | 17 | 96 |
| 4 | 26 | 105 |
| 5 | 18 | 112 |

## Grade K Language—Lesson 75

Lesson 75 from Grade K Language includes material from the following components:

- Language Presentation Book B
- Workbook

You begin Lesson 75 by presenting oral exercises on verb tenses, materials, and common locations (exercises 1–3). Then students look at pictures in the Presentation Book as you present exercises on classification, common information, and concept application (exercises 4–7). You also present an exercise that reviews previously taught part/whole concepts (exercise 8).

For the next part of the lesson, students complete Workbook activities that involve pair relations, classification, part/whole, opposites, and concept application. When students finish, you read the story "Dozy at the Zoo," which appears at the back of the Presentation Book. Finally, you present one or more of the Expanded Language Activities.

# LESSON 75

## ★ EXERCISE 1 Actions—Verb Tense/Pronouns

**1.** It's time for some actions.

**a.** Everybody, point to the wall. (Signal. Wait.)
What are you doing? (Signal.) *Pointing to the wall.*
Everybody, point to a window. (Signal. Wait.)
What are you doing? (Signal.) *Pointing to a window.*

**b.** What were you doing? (Signal.) *Pointing to the wall.*
Say the whole thing. (Signal.) *I was pointing to the wall.*
(Have children stop pointing to the window.)

**c.** (Repeat part 1 until all children's responses are firm.)

**2.** I'm going to call on three children.

**a.** (Call on three children.) _____, _____, and _____, point to a window.
Everybody, what are they doing? (Signal.) *Pointing to a window.*

**b.** _____, _____, and _____, point to a wall.
Everybody, what are they doing? (Signal.) *Pointing to a wall.*
What were they doing? (Signal.) *Pointing to a window.*
Say the whole thing about what they were doing. (Signal.) *They were pointing to a window.*
(Have children stop pointing to a wall.)

**c.** (Repeat part 2 until all children's responses are firm.)

**3.** Let's do another one.

**a.** Everybody, point to the window. (Signal. Wait.)
What are you doing? (Signal.) *Pointing to the window.*
Everybody, point to the wall. (Signal. Wait.)
What are you doing? (Signal.) *Pointing to the wall.*

**b.** What were you doing? (Signal.) *Pointing to the window.*
Say the whole thing. (Signal.) *I was pointing to the window.*

**c.** What are you doing? (Signal.) *Pointing to the wall.*
Say the whole thing. (Signal.) *I am pointing to the wall.*
(Have children stop pointing to the wall.)

**d.** (Repeat part 3 until all children's responses are firm.)

## ★ EXERCISE 2 Materials

**1.** Think of things that are made of wood. Let's see who can name at least three things made of wood.
(Call on different children to name objects made of wood. Each child should name at least three things.)

**2.** Think of things that are made of cloth. Let's see who can name at least three things made of cloth.
(Call on different children to name objects made of cloth. Each child should name at least three things.)

**3.** Think of things that are made of plastic. Let's see who can name at least three things made of plastic.
(Call on different children to name objects made of plastic. Each child should name at least three things.)

## ★ EXERCISE 3 Common Information

**1.** Let's see how much information you remember.

**a.** What do we call a place with lots of people? (Signal.) *A city.*
Say the whole thing about a city. (Signal.) *A city is a place with lots of people.*

**b.** What do we call a place where food is grown? (Signal.) *A farm.*
Say the whole thing about a farm. (Signal.) *A farm is a place where food is grown.*

**c.** What do we call a place where you buy things? (Signal.) *A store.*
Say the whole thing about a store. (Signal.) *A store is a place where you buy things.*

**2.** (Repeat part 1 until all children's responses are firm.)

### Individual Turns
(Repeat the exercise, calling on different children for each step.)

263

Lesson 75

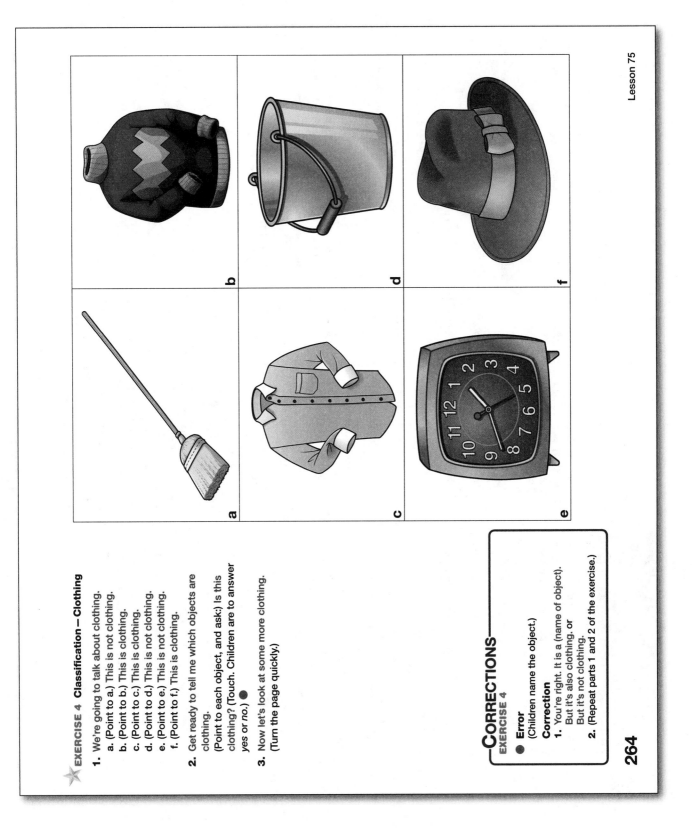

a

b

c

d

e

f

⭐ **EXERCISE 4 Classification — Clothing**

1. We're going to talk about clothing.
   a. (Point to a.) This is not clothing.
   b. (Point to b.) This is clothing.
   c. (Point to c.) This is clothing.
   d. (Point to d.) This is not clothing.
   e. (Point to e.) This is not clothing.
   f. (Point to f.) This is clothing.

2. Get ready to tell me which objects are clothing.
   (Point to each object, and ask:) Is this clothing? (Touch. Children are to answer *yes* or *no*.) ●

3. Now let's look at some more clothing.
   (Turn the page quickly.)

## CORRECTIONS
### EXERCISE 4

● **Error**
   (Children name the object.)

**Correction**
1. You're right. It is a (name of object).
   But it's also clothing. or
   But it's not clothing.
2. (Repeat parts 1 and 2 of the exercise.)

**264**

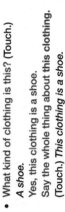

b

d

a

c

Lesson 75

**EXERCISE 4 Classification – Clothing (cont.)**

**4.** (Point to each article of clothing, and say:)
This is clothing.

**a.** (Point to a.)
Is this clothing? (Touch.) *Yes.*
Say the whole thing. (Touch.) *This is clothing.*

- What kind of clothing is this? (Touch.)
*A sock.*
Yes, this clothing is a sock.
Say the whole thing about this clothing.
(Touch.) *This clothing is a sock.*

**b.** (Point to b.)
Is this clothing? (Touch.) *Yes.*
Say the whole thing. (Touch.) *This is clothing.*

- What kind of clothing is this? (Touch.)
*A shirt.*
Yes, this clothing is a shirt.
Say the whole thing about this clothing.
(Touch.) *This clothing is a shirt.*

**c.** (Point to c.)
Is this clothing? (Touch.) *Yes.*
Say the whole thing. (Touch.) *This is clothing.*

- What kind of clothing is this? (Touch.)
*A sweater.*
Yes, this clothing is a sweater.
Say the whole thing about this clothing.
(Touch.) *This clothing is a sweater.*

**d.** (Point to d.)
Is this clothing? (Touch.) *Yes.*
Say the whole thing. (Touch.) *This is clothing.*

- What kind of clothing is this? (Touch.)
*A shoe.*
Yes, this clothing is a shoe.
Say the whole thing about this clothing.
(Touch.) *This clothing is a shoe.*

**5.** (Repeat part 4 until all children's responses are firm.)

**Individual Turns**
(Repeat part 4, calling on different children for each step.)

265

Lesson 75

**EXERCISE 5  Common Information**

1. Look at the picture. It shows the land and the sky. I'll touch parts of the picture. Tell me if I touch things on land or in the sky.
   a. (Touch the sky.) Am I touching the land or the sky? (Touch.) *The sky.*
   b. (Touch the land.) Am I touching the land or the sky? (Touch.) *The land.*
   c. (Repeat steps a and b until all children's responses are firm.)

2. Watch.
   a. (Touch the clouds.) What am I touching in the sky? (Touch.) *Clouds.*
      Yes, clouds are in the sky.
   b. (Touch the sun.) What am I touching? (Touch.) *The sun.*
      Yes, the sun is in the sky.
   c. (Repeat steps a and b until all children's responses are firm.)

3. Watch.
   a. (Touch the trees.) What am I touching on the land? (Touch.) *Trees.*
      Yes, trees grow on the land.
   b. (Touch the river.) What am I touching? (Touch.) *A river.*
      Yes, rivers are on the land.
   c. (Repeat steps a and b until all children's responses are firm.)

4. One more time. I'll touch things in the picture. You tell me if they are on the land or in the sky.
   a. (Touch each object, and ask:) Do you find this on the land or in the sky? (Children are to answer *land* or *sky.*)
   b. (Repeat step a until all children's responses are firm.)

266

★ **EXERCISE 6  Concept Application**

**1.** You're going to figure out a problem about a goat and some flowers.

The goat will jump over only some of these flowers. Here's the rule: The goat will jump over the flowers with leaves.

Everybody, say the rule. (Signal.) *The goat will jump over the flowers with leaves.*

Again. (Signal.) *The goat will jump over the flowers with leaves.*

(Repeat until all children can say the rule.)

**2.** Now answer these questions.

**a.** (Point to a.) Do these flowers have leaves? (Touch.) *Yes.*

So what do you know about these flowers? (Call on a child. Idea: *The goat will jump over these flowers.*)

You're right. The goat will jump over the flowers with leaves.

**b.** (Point to b.) Do these flowers have leaves? (Touch.) *No.*

So what do you know about these flowers? (Call on a child. Idea: *The goat won't jump over these flowers.*)

You're right. The goat won't jump over these flowers.

**3.** Everybody, what's the rule? (Signal.) *The goat will jump over the flowers with leaves.*

**a.** (Point to a.) Do these flowers have leaves? (Touch.) *Yes.*

So what do you know about these flowers? (Call on a child. Idea: *The goat will jump over these flowers.*)

You're right. The goat will jump over these flowers.

**b.** (Point to b.) Do these flowers have leaves? (Touch.) *No.*

So what do you know about these flowers? (Call on a child. Idea: *The goat won't jump over these flowers.*)

You're right. The goat won't jump over these flowers.

**4.** (Call on two children.)

• Show me the flowers that the goat will jump over. (Wait.)

• Let's see if you're right. (Turn the page quickly.)

267

Lesson 75

**EXERCISE 6  Concept Application (cont.)**

**5.**  Answer these questions.

a.  (Point to a.) Do these flowers have leaves? (Touch.) *Yes.*

What is the goat doing? (Call on a child. Idea: *Jumping over the flowers with leaves.*)

You're right. The goat is jumping over the flowers with leaves.

Everybody, say the whole thing about what the goat is doing. (Touch.) *The goat is jumping over the flowers with leaves.*

b.  (Point to b.) Do these flowers have leaves? (Touch.) *No.*

Is the goat jumping over these flowers? (Touch.) *No.*

What is jumping over these flowers? (Touch.) *A frog.*

c.  (Repeat part 5 until all children's responses are firm.)

**6.**  (Call on different children.)

•  Why do you think the goat and the frog look happy?

•  Which flowers do you think the goat would like to eat?

•  Which animal do you think can jump the highest? Why?

**Individual Turns**
(Repeat part 5, calling on different children for each step.)

**268**

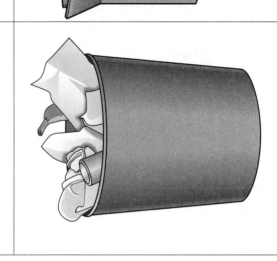

⭐ **EXERCISE 7  Classification—Containers**

1. We're going to learn a rule about containers. (Point to each container, and ask:) What kind of container is this? (Touch. Children are to answer *a basket, a suitcase, a wastebasket, a box.*)

2. Here's the rule about all containers.
   a. Listen. If you put things in it, it's a container. Listen again. If you put things in it, it's a container. Everybody, say the rule. (Signal.) *If you put things in it, it's a container.*
   b. Again. (Signal.) *If you put things in it, it's a container.*
   c. (Repeat step b until all children can say the rule.)

3. Now let's look at the objects on the next page.
   (Turn the page quickly.)

**269**

Lesson 75

b

d

a

c

**EXERCISE 7   Classification — Containers (cont.)**

4. **a.** (Point to a.) Do you put things in this? (Touch.) *Yes.*

   If you put things in it, it's a . . . (touch) *container.*

   You put things in a bag. So what do you know about a bag? (Touch.) *It's a container.*

   • Again. What do you know about a bag? (Touch.) *It's a container.*

   **b.** (Point to b.) Do you put things in this? (Touch.) *No.*

   You cannot put things in a ball. So what do you know about a ball? (Touch.) *It's not a container.*

   • Again. What do you know about a ball? (Touch.) *It's not a container.*

   **c.** (Point to c.) Do you put things in this? (Touch.) *No.*

   You cannot put things in a flower. So what do you know about a flower? (Touch.) *It's not a container.*

   • Again. What do you know about a flower? (Touch.) *It's not a container.*

   **d.** (Point to d.) Do you put things in this? (Touch.) *Yes.*

   If you put things in it, it's a . . . (touch) *container.*

   You put things in a wastebasket. So what do you know about a wastebasket? (Touch.) *It's a container.*

   • Again. What do you know about a wastebasket? (Touch.) *It's a container.*

   • (Repeat step d until all children's responses are firm.)

5. (Repeat part 4 until all children's responses are firm.)

270

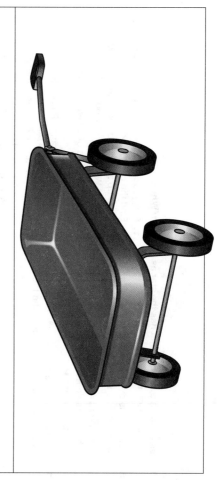

Lesson 75

**EXERCISE 8  Part/Whole – Umbrella, Wagon**

Let's see if you remember the parts of these objects.

1. Get ready to tell me the parts of an umbrella. Say the whole thing.
   a. (Point to the frame. Pause. Touch.)
      *An umbrella has a frame.*
      (Point to the handle. Pause. Touch.)
      *An umbrella has a handle.*
      (Point to the covering. Pause. Touch.)
      *An umbrella has a covering.*
   b. (Repeat step a until all children's responses are firm.)
   c. (Circle the umbrella.) And what do you call the whole object? (Pause. Touch.)
      *An umbrella.*
      And what do we usually do with an umbrella? (Touch. Praise reasonable responses.)

2. Get ready to tell me the parts of a wagon. Say the whole thing.
   a. (Point to the frame. Pause. Touch.)
      *A wagon has a frame.*
      (Point to the handle. Pause. Touch.)
      *A wagon has a handle.*
      (Point to the body. Pause. Touch.)
      *A wagon has a body.*
      (Point to the wheels. Pause. Touch.)
      *A wagon has wheels.*
   b. (Repeat step a until all children's responses are firm.)
   c. (Circle the wagon.) And what do you call the whole object? (Touch.) *A wagon.*
      And what do we usually do with a wagon? (Touch. Praise reasonable responses.)

**Individual Turns**
(Repeat the exercise, calling on different children for each step.)

**271**

**WORKBOOK LESSON 75**

**Pair Relations**

**1.** Find the box with the star and a moon. ✔
The boxes at the top show what the other boxes should look like.

**a.** Touch the first box at the top. ✔
What are the objects in that box? (Signal.) *A star and a moon.*

**b.** Touch the next box at the top. ✔
What are the objects in that box? (Signal.) *A broom and a door.*

**2.** There's something missing in all the other boxes. You're going to make some of the boxes look like the boxes on top. You're going to cross out the boxes that are wrong.

**3.** Listen: You can fix a box if the first object is either a star or a broom. Again, a star or a broom.

**a.** What does the first object have to be? (Signal.) *A star or a broom.*

**b.** Can you fix it if the first object is a star? (Signal.) *Yes.*
Can you fix it if the first object is a broom? (Signal.) *Yes.*
Can you fix it if the first object is a tree? (Signal.) *No.*
Can you fix it if the first object is a cake? (Signal.) *No.*
Can you fix it if the first object is a star? (Signal.) *Yes.*
Yes, the first object has to be a star or a broom.

**4.** Listen: Circle every box that has the star as the first object. ✔

**5.** Listen: Circle every box that has a broom as the first object. ✔

**6.** Listen: Cross out every box that is not circled. Those boxes do not have a star or a broom as the first object. ✔

**7.** Later you'll fix all the boxes you circled so they are like one of the boxes at the top.

**Classification**

**1.** Find the triangle. ✔
(Hold up the workbook.) Some of these objects are vehicles.
(Point to each object, and ask:) Is this a vehicle?
(Children are to answer *yes* or *no*.)

**2.** Listen: The objects that are vehicles should be in the triangle.

**a.** Where should the vehicles be? (Signal.) *In the triangle.*

**b.** Draw a red line from each object that is a vehicle to the triangle. Don't draw lines for objects that are not vehicles. ✔

**3.** You have the vehicles in the triangle.
The rest of the objects belong in the house.
Draw black lines for those objects. ✔

**4.** You have the vehicles in the triangle and the rest of the objects in the house. Good for you.

**Part/Whole**

**1.** Everybody, turn your workbook page over.
Find the pencils. ✔
(Hold up the workbook. Point to the whole pencil.) What is this? (Touch.) *A pencil.*

**2.** Name the parts of a pencil. Say the whole thing.

**a.** (Point to the point. Pause. Touch.) *A pencil has a point.*

**b.** (Point to the shaft. Pause. Touch.) *A pencil has a shaft.*

**c.** (Point to the eraser. Pause. Touch.) *A pencil has an eraser.*

**3.** Some of these pencils do not have erasers.

**a.** Here are the erasers. (Point to the separate erasers.)

**b.** Draw lines from the pencils to the erasers. ✔

**4.** Later you'll color the pencils.

## WORKBOOK
### LESSON 75 CONTINUED

**Opposites**

1. Find the snakes. ✔

2. Circle the snakes that are not long. ✔

3. Here's a rule for the snakes that are not long:
   The snakes that are not long should be green.
   a. What color should those snakes be?
      (Signal.) *Green.*
   b. Make a green mark on one of the snakes
      you circled. ✔

4. Later you'll color those snakes green.

**Concept Application**

1. Find the fence. ✔

2. Here is the rule for this picture: The dog with
   the bone is wet.
   Which dog is wet? (Signal.) *The dog with the
   bone.*

3. Circle the dog that is wet. Make some water
   drops on that dog. ✔

4. Cross out the dogs that are not wet. ✔

Reread "Dozy at the Zoo" in Storybook 2,
page 31.

See Additional Language Activities on
the Lessons 71–75 Planning Page.

273

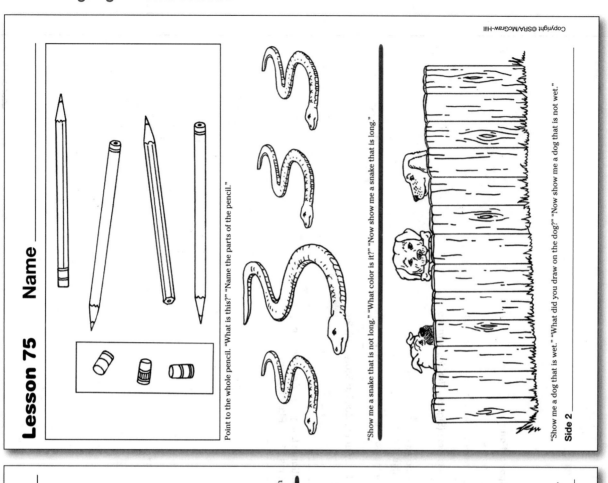

## Lesson 75    Name _____

Point to the whole pencil. "What is this?" "Name the parts of the pencil."

"Show me a snake that is not long." "What color is it?" "Now show me a snake that is long."

"Show me a dog that is wet." "What did you draw on the dog?" "Now show me a dog that is not wet."
**Side 2**

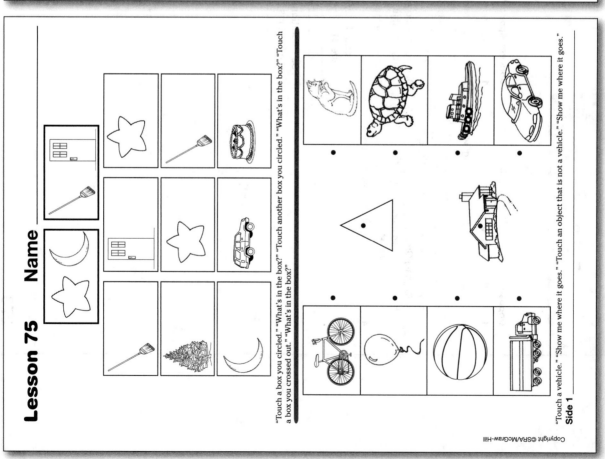

## Lesson 75    Name _____

"Touch a box you circled." "What's in the box?" "Touch another box you circled." "What's in the box?" "Touch a box you crossed out." "What's in the box?"

"Touch a vehicle." "Show me where it goes." "Touch an object that is not a vehicle." "Show me where it goes."
**Side 1**

**Dozy at the Zoo**

**31**

(Read this story after finishing lesson 74.)

**DOZY AT THE ZOO**
Prepositions

One night Dozy had a dream. He dreamed that he worked in the zoo. In his dream he fed the lions and the monkeys and the elephants and the seals.

Dozy at the Zoo

32

In his dream, Dozy met a zookeeper. She came up to him and said, "Put this baby lion in the cage."

Everybody, what did the zookeeper say? (Signal.) *"Put this baby lion in the cage."* Where did the zookeeper say to put the baby lion? (Signal.) *In the cage.*

"Okay," Dozy said. Do you think Dozy will do what the zookeeper said? (Call on different children.)
Let's find out.

Then the zookeeper put the baby lion in the cage. She said, "Now the baby lion is in the cage."

Look at Dozy. He does not look happy.

Look what Dozy did. Where did Dozy put the baby lion? (Signal.) *On the cage.*

The zookeeper said, "Is the baby lion in the cage? No, the baby lion is not in the cage. The baby lion is on the cage. Dozy, you are not thinking."

**Dozy at the Zoo**

**33**

Dozy at the Zoo

**34**

Next in the dream the zookeeper gave Dozy a long rope. She said, "The monkeys like to play with the rope. So put this rope over the monkey pond."

Where did the zookeeper say to put the rope? (Signal.) *Over the monkey pond.*

"Okay," Dozy said. Do you think Dozy will do what the zookeeper said? (Call on different children.)
Let's find out.

# Grade K Language Presentation Book Story

Dozy went to the monkey pond, and look what he did with the rope.

Where did Dozy put the rope?
(Signal.) *In the pond.*
Where did the zookeeper say to put the rope?
(Signal.) *Over the pond.*

The zookeeper said, "The rope is not over the monkey pond. The rope is in the monkey pond. Dozy, you are not thinking."

The zookeeper put the rope over the pond. She said, "Now the rope is over the pond."

**35**

Dozy at the Zoo

In Dozy's dream the zookeeper said, "The lions are hungry. They like meat. So we will put this meat next to the lions' cage. We cannot go in the cage."

"Okay," Dozy said. Do you think Dozy heard what the zookeeper said? **(Call on different children.)**
Let's find out.

36

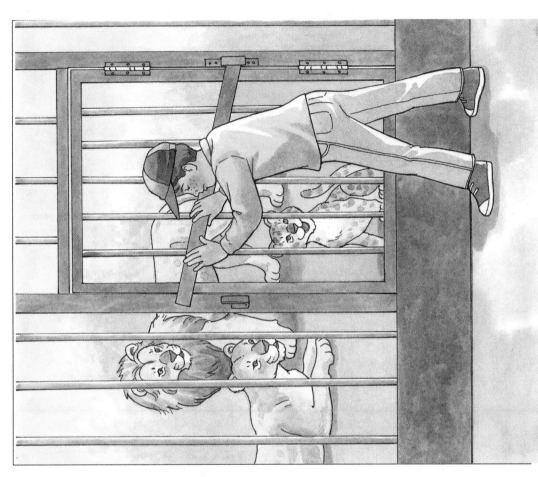

Dozy at the Zoo

37

In his dream Dozy went up to the lions' cage.
He started to open the door to the cage.
Watch out, you sleepy Dozy! Those lions will get you!

Dozy at the Zoo

The zookeeper came running up and pulled Dozy away from the cage door.

She said, "I said to put the meat next to the cage. Not in the cage. Dozy, you are not listening."

38

# Grade K Language Presentation Book Story

Then in the dream the zookeeper gave Dozy a great big bucket of water. She said, "Dozy, if you don't listen to me, you won't be able to help me anymore."

Dozy liked to help the zookeeper. So he really tried to listen. Do you think he will hear her? (Call on different children.)

The zookeeper said, "The elephants are thirsty. They want water. Let's put this bucket of water in the elephant cage."

Everybody, where did the zookeeper say to put the water? (Signal.) *In the elephant cage.*

"Okay," Dozy said. Do you think Dozy will do what the zookeeper said? (Call on different children.)
Let's find out.

**39**

Dozy took the bucket of water. He walked up to the elephant cage and reached inside. He put the bucket of water down.

Where is the bucket of water? (Signal.) *In the cage.*

Is Dozy doing what the zookeeper said to do? (Signal.) *Yes.*

The zookeeper said, "The bucket of water is in the elephant cage. Dozy, you are listening."

The elephant was very thirsty. She drank and drank and drank.

In Dozy's dream, the zookeeper brought the elephant out. Then the elephant picked up Dozy with her trunk. And where do you think the elephant put Dozy? (Call on different children.)

40

Dozy at the Zoo

**Dozy at the Zoo**

But then Dozy woke up. He was not on the elephant. He was in his bed. He said, "Where is the elephant? Where are the baby lions? Where is the big lion? Where are the monkeys? What a good dream I had."

(Call on different children to answer these questions.)

How would riding on top of an elephant make you feel?

Tell about some of the things Dozy did at the zoo.

What would you like to do at a zoo?

41

# Expanded Language Activities

These Expanded Language Activities are to be used at the end of the designated lessons.

## LESSONS 51–55

- Teach children Getting Hotter . . . Getting Colder. Have one child face the wall while another child points to an object in the classroom. Then tell the first child to turn around and the other children to give clues for locating the object by shouting "getting hotter" or "getting colder" to direct the child to the target object.

- Teach children the finger play:
  *Open, shut them, open, shut them, give a little clap.*
  *Open, shut them, open, shut them, put them in your lap.*
  *Creep them, creep them, right up to your chin.*
  *Open wide your little mouth, but do not let them in.*
  *Open, shut them, open, shut them, give a little clap.*
  *Open, shut them, open, shut them, put them in your lap.*

- Teach a poem:
  Children learn two familiar nursery rhymes.

## LESSONS 56–60

- Children sing "What Is Your Name?"

- Make a simple treasure hunt for children to follow. Children work in teams of three or four. Each team needs a list of pictures showing objects they are to find. A prize can be awarded to the winning team.

- Teach children to play Concentration.

## LESSONS 61–65

- Teach children the finger play Where is Thumbkin?

- Children make Action Booklets by pasting (or drawing) action pictures of people and animals onto folded paper. Children tell what the people and animals are doing.

- Teach children to play the game What Am I Thinking Of? Start by giving them one piece of information. For example, say I am thinking of something in this classroom. What am I thinking of? Call on three children. If no one answers correctly, give another piece of information. For example, say You use this thing to write with. Then call on three different children. Continue this pattern until children have given the correct answer.

## LESSONS 66–70

- Children make Object Booklets by pasting (or drawing) pictures of objects onto folded paper. Each child tells the other children the names of the objects in their books.

- Children do the finger play Where is Thumbkin?

- Children begin work on a Classification Scrapbook. Have them cut out and paste (or draw) pictures of vehicles onto construction paper. Set these pages aside. Children will add additional pages to their scrapbooks as they learn different classifications.

- Play the game What Am I Thinking Of? Use objects in the room and objects from the different classifications children are learning; also use opposites.

## LESSONS 71–75

- Bring objects from home or have magazine cut-outs to show the children. Ask children: What color is it? What do you use it for?

- Play the guessing game What Am I Thinking Of?

- Children play Color Fish and Lotto.

Expanded Language Activities

v

## Grade 1 Language Arts— Lesson 12

Lesson 12 from Grade 1 Language Arts includes material from the following components:

- Language Arts Presentation Book A
- Workbook

You begin Lesson 12 by presenting oral exercises on actions, classification, *where,* opposites, calendar facts, and same-different (exercises 1–6). Then you present a calendar and have students identify today's date and yesterday's date (exercise 7). Next you read students a story (exercise 8) and have them color a Workbook picture of the story (exercise 9). Finally, students complete Workbook exercises on part-whole and location (exercises 10 and 11).

## LESSON 12

### Objectives

- **Label actions, and follow directions involving "all," "some" and "none," and** generate complete sentences to describe an action and answer questions involving "or." (Exercise 1)
- Identify classes and name members of those classes. (Exercise 2)
- Identify statements that tell "where" and generate statements that tell "where" and statements that tell "where something is not." (Exercise 3)
- Answer questions by generating sentences using opposites. (Exercise 4)
- Answer questions about previously learned calendar facts. (Exercise 5)
- Name ways that two common objects are the same and/or different. (Exercise 6)
- Given a calendar, identify the day and date for "yesterday" and "today." (Exercise 7)
- Answer questions about a new story. (Exercise 8)
- Make a picture consistent with the details of the story. (Exercise 9)
- Follow coloring rules involving parts of a whole. (Exercise 10)
- Follow coloring rules involving class. (Exercise 11)

### EXERCISE 1  Actions

1. Watch me. Tell if I hold up **all of my fingers** or **some of my fingers** or **none of my fingers.**
2. (Hold up ten fingers.) Is this all of my fingers or some of my fingers or none of my fingers? (Signal.) *All of your fingers.*
- (Hold up two fists.) Is this all of my fingers or some of my fingers or none of my fingers? (Signal.) *None of your fingers.*
- (Hold up three fingers.) Is this all of my fingers or some of my fingers or none of my fingers? (Signal.) *Some of your fingers.*
3. Now it's your turn. Everybody, hold up none of your fingers. Get ready. (Signal.) ✔
- What are you holding up? (Signal.) *None of my fingers.*
- Say the whole thing. Get ready. (Signal.) *I am holding up none of my fingers.*
4. Everybody, hold up all of your fingers. (Signal.) ✔
- What are you holding up? (Signal.) *All of my fingers.*
- Say the whole thing. Get ready. (Signal.) *I am holding up all of my fingers.*
5. (Repeat steps 3 and 4 until firm.)
6. Let's try another game. I'm going to do something. See if you can figure out what I'm going to do.

7. Listen: I'm going to stamp my foot or stamp my feet or stand up. What am I going to do? (Signal.) *Stamp your foot or stamp your feet or stand up.*
8. (Repeat step 7 until firm.)
9. Yes, I'm going to stamp my foot or stamp my feet or stand up. Am I going to stand up? (Signal.) *Maybe.*
- Am I going to stamp my feet? (Signal.) *Maybe.*
- Am I going to stamp my foot? (Signal.) *Maybe.*
- Am I going to sing? (Signal.) *No.*
10. I'm going to stamp my foot or stamp my feet or stand up. What am I going to do? (Signal.) *Stamp your foot or stamp your feet or stand up.*
11. Here I go. (Stamp both feet.) Did I stand up? (Signal.) *No.*
- Did I stamp my feet? (Signal.) *Yes.*
- Did I sit down? (Signal.) *No.*
12. What did I do? (Signal.) *Stamped your feet.*
- Say the whole thing. Get ready. (Signal.) *You stamped your feet.*
13. (Repeat step 12 until firm.)
14. (Repeat steps 11 through 13 until firm.)

### EXERCISE 2  Classification

1. I'm going to name some objects. Tell me a class these objects are in. (Accept all reasonable responses, but then suggest the response given.)

**62**   *Lesson 12*

2. Listen: spaghetti, beans, ice cream, salad. Everybody, what class? (Signal.) *Food.* Yes, food.
- Listen: school, garage, house, restaurant. Everybody, what class? (Signal.) *Buildings.* Yes, buildings.
- Listen: ax, hoe, hammer, screwdriver, shovel. Everybody, what class? (Signal.) *Tools.* Yes, tools.
3. (Repeat step 2 until firm.)
4. I'm going to name a class. See how many objects you can name in that class. Listen: food. (Call on individual children. Accept all reasonable responses.)
- I'm going to name another class. See how many objects you can name in that class. Listen: buildings. (Call on individual children. Accept all reasonable responses.)
- I'm going to name another class. See how many objects you can name in that class. Listen: tools. (Call on individual children. Accept all reasonable responses.)

### EXERCISE 3   Where

1. I'm going to say statements. Some of these statements tell where the bicycle is. Some of these statements don't tell where the bicycle is.
2. Listen: The bicycle is in the street. Say the statement. Get ready. (Signal.) *The bicycle is in the street.*
- Does that statement tell where the bicycle is? (Signal.) *Yes.*
- Where is the bicycle? (Signal.) *In the street.*
3. Listen: The bicycle is wet. Say the statement. Get ready. (Signal.) *The bicycle is wet.*
- Does that statement tell where the bicycle is? (Signal.) *No.*
4. (Repeat steps 2 and 3 until firm.)
5. Now it's your turn to make up statements. Make up a statement that tells **where** the bicycle is. (Call on individual children. Praise good statements.)
- Make up a statement that does **not** tell where the bicycle is. (Call on individual children. Praise good statements.)

### EXERCISE 4   Opposites

**Review**

1. We're going to play a word game.
2. Listen: I'm thinking about trees that are not wet. They're not wet. So what else do you know about them? (Signal.) *They're dry.*
- Listen: I'm thinking of a rabbit that is fat. It's fat. So what else do you know about it? (Signal.) *It's not skinny.*
- Listen: I'm thinking of a woman who is not old. She's not old. So what else do you know about her? (Signal.) *She's young.*
- Listen: I'm thinking about a log that is long. It's long. So what else do you know about it? (Signal.) *It's not short.*
3. (Repeat step 2 until firm.)

### EXERCISE 5   Calendar Facts

1. Everybody, how many days are in a week? (Signal.) *Seven.*
- Say the fact. Get ready. (Signal.) *There are seven days in a week.*
- Everybody, say the days of the week. Get ready. (Signal.) *Sunday, Monday, Tuesday, Wednesday, Thursday, Friday, Saturday.*
2. How many months are in a year? (Signal.) *12.*
- Say the fact. Get ready. (Signal.) *There are 12 months in a year.*
3. Name the months of the year through December. Get ready. (Signal.) *January, February, March, April, May, June, July, August, September, October, November, December.*
4. (Repeat step 3 until firm.)
5. Everybody, how many seasons are in a year? (Signal.) *Four.*
- Say the seasons of the year. Get ready. (Signal.) *Winter, spring, summer, fall.*
6. (Repeat step 5 until firm.)

### EXERCISE 6   Same-Different

1. We're going to talk about how things are the same and how they are different.
2. Listen: a chair and a table. See if you can name two ways they are the same. (Call on individual children. Have the group repeat each correct answer. Then say:) You told me how a chair and a table are . . . (Signal.) *the same.*

*Lesson 12*   **63**

- Listen: a chair and a table. See if you can name two ways they are different. (Call on individual children. Have the group repeat each correct answer. Then say:) You told me how a chair and a table are . . . (Signal.) *different.*

3. Here's another one. Listen: ice cream and snow. See if you can name two ways they are the same. (Call on individual children. Have the group repeat each correct answer. Then say:) You told me how ice cream and snow are . . . (Signal.) *the same.*

- Listen: ice cream and snow. See if you can name two ways they are different. (Call on individual children. Have the group repeat each correct answer. Then say:) You told me how ice cream and snow are . . . (Signal.) *different.*

### EXERCISE 7   Calendar

1. (Present calendar.) First you'll tell me about the days of the week. Then you'll tell me about the dates.
2. Tell me the day of the week it was yesterday. Get ready. (Signal.)
- Tell me the day of the week it is today. Get ready. (Signal.)
- Now the dates. Everybody, tell me yesterday's date. Get ready. (Signal.)
- Tell me today's date. Get ready. (Signal.)
3. (Repeat step 2 until firm.)

### EXERCISE 8   The Bragging Rats Race

**Storytelling**

- Everybody, I'm going to read you a story. Listen to the things that happen in the story because you're going to have to fix up a picture that shows part of the story. This is a story about some rats. Listen:

A bunch of rats lived near a pond that was on a farm. The rats got along well, except for two of them. The other rats called these two the bragging rats because they were always bragging, quarreling and arguing about something.

One day they'd argue about who could eat the most. Another day they'd squabble and quarrel over who was the best looking. Neither one of them was very good looking. One was a big gray rat with the longest tail you've ever seen on a rat. The other one wasn't big, but he had the biggest, yellowest teeth you ever saw.

- Listen to the last part again and get a picture in your mind of those rats.

One was a big gray rat with the longest tail you've ever seen on a rat. The other one wasn't big, but he had the biggest, yellowest teeth you ever saw.

- What was unusual about the big gray rat? (Call on a child. Idea: *It had the longest tail you've ever seen on a rat.*)
- What was unusual about the other rat? (Call on a child. Idea: *It had the biggest, yellowest teeth you ever saw.*)
- What are some of the things these two would argue about? (Call on a child. Ideas: *Who was the best looking; who could eat the most.*)

The other rats in the bunch didn't pay much attention to the bragging and quarreling until the two rats started bragging about who was the fastest rat in the whole bunch. This quarrel went on for days, and the other rats got pretty sick of listening to the rats shout and yell and brag about how fast they were.

- Listen: What were the two bragging rats arguing about? (Call on a child. Idea: *Who was the fastest rat.*)

On the third day of their quarrel, they almost got into a fight. The rat with the yellow teeth was saying, "I'm so fast that I could run circles around you while you ran as fast as you could."

The big rat said, "Oh, yeah? Well, I could run circles around your circles. That's how fast I am."

- Are these rats kind of silly? (Call on a child. Accept reasonable responses.)

The two rats continued yelling at each other until a wise old rat said, "Stop! We are tired of listening to all this shouting and yelling and bragging. There is a way to find out who is the fastest rat on this farm."

- How could they find out who was the fastest? (Call on a child. Idea: *Have a race.*)

The wise old rat continued, "We will have a race for any rat that wants to race. Everybody will line up, run down the path to the pond, then run back. The first rat to get back is the winner. And then we'll have no more arguing about which rat is the fastest."

- Get a picture in your mind of how they're going to run. They'll start at the starting line, run down the path to the pond, turn around at the pond and run all the way back to the starting line. The wise old rat said there would be no more arguing about who could run the fastest.
- Why wouldn't there be any more arguing about which rat was the fastest? (Call on a child. Idea: *Because the race would prove who was the fastest.*)

The rats agreed, and early the next morning they were lined up, ready for the big race. Six rats entered the race. The bragging rats were lined up right next to each other, making mean faces and mumbling about how fast they were going to run.

The rats put their noses close to the ground, ready to take off like a flash. "Everybody, steady," the wise old rat said. "Everybody, ready. Go!" The rats took off toward the pond. The big gray rat got ahead of the others, with the yellow-toothed rat right behind him. But just before they got to the pond, the yellow-toothed rat stepped on the long tail of the gray rat, and both rats tumbled over and over in a cloud of dust.

- Listen: Why did the two rats start tumbling? (Call on a child. Idea: *Because the yellow-toothed rat stepped on the long tail of the gray rat.*)

- Where were they when this accident took place? (Call on a child. Idea: *Almost to the pond.*)
- I wonder if something bad is going to happen. Let's see.

The two bragging rats tumbled down the dusty path and right into the pond.

The other rats finished the race. The winner was a little black rat. It was hard for her to finish the race because she was laughing so hard over the bragging rats who were still splashing and sputtering around in the pond.

After the race, all the other rats went back to the pond. The bragging rats were still splashing and sputtering. The wise old rat said to them, "So now we know who the fastest runner on this farm is. It's neither one of you, so we will have no more arguments from either of you about who can run the fastest!"

- Listen: Who won the race? (Call on a child. Idea: *A little black rat.*)
- Do you think the bragging rats will stop arguing about who is the fastest? (Call on a child. Accept reasonable responses.)
- Let's see.

The bragging rats looked at each other. Then the rat with yellow teeth suddenly smiled and said, "I may not be the fastest **runner** in this bunch, but there is no rat in the world that can **swim** as fast as I can."

"Oh, yeah?" said the gray rat.

"I can swim so fast that I could go all the way across the pond without even getting my fur wet."

The wise old rat and the other rats just walked away from the pond, slowly shaking their heads.

- Why do you think they were shaking their heads? (Call on a child. Idea: *The race didn't settle anything.*)
- I don't think these bragging rats will ever stop bragging and arguing.

*Lesson 12* **65**

## WORKBOOK

### EXERCISE 9  Story Details

**The Bragging Rats**

1. Everybody, open your workbook to Lesson 12. Write your name at the top of the page. ✔
2. This picture shows something that happened in the story. Where are the bragging rats? (Call on a child. Idea: *In the pond.*)
- Everybody, do those rats look very happy? (Signal.) *No.*
- Is the race still going on when this picture takes place? (Signal.) *No.*
- How do you know the race is over? (Call on a child. Idea: *All the other rats are laughing at the bragging rats in the pond.*)
- See if you can find the rat that ended up winning the race. Remember, that's a little black rat. ✔
- See if you can find the wise old rat. That's the oldest-looking rat in the picture. ✔
3. Everybody, take out a yellow crayon and a gray crayon. ✔
- Listen: Put a little yellow mark on the teeth of the rat that had yellow teeth. Then put a little gray mark on the other bragging rat. Later you can color this picture.

### EXERCISE 10  Part-Whole

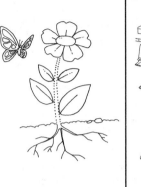

1. Everybody, find the next page in your workbook. (Hold up a workbook.) Your page should look just like mine. ✔
2. Touch the first part of your page. (Point to the first half of the page.) You should be touching this part of your page. ✔
3. Find the flower. ✔
4. Here's a coloring rule for the flower. Listen: Color the petals red. What's the rule? (Signal.) *Color the petals red.*
- Mark the petals. ✔
5. Here's another coloring rule for the flower. Listen: Color the roots brown. What's the rule? (Signal.) *Color the roots brown.*
- Mark the roots. ✔
6. Here's another coloring rule for the flower. Listen: Color the leaves green. What's the rule? (Signal.) *Color the leaves green.*
- Mark the leaves. ✔
7. Part of the flower is missing. What part is missing? (Signal.) *The stem.* Yes, the stem.
- Before you color the flower, you're going to follow the dots and make the stem.
8. Here's the coloring rule for the stem. Listen: Color the stem orange. What's the rule? (Signal.) *Color the stem orange.*
- Mark the stem. ✔

### EXERCISE 11   Location

1. (Hold up your workbook. Point to second half.)
2. Everybody, what place do you see in this picture? (Signal.) *An airport.*
3. Here's a coloring rule for this picture. Listen: Color all vehicles yellow. What's the rule? (Signal.) *Color all vehicles yellow.*
   * (Repeat step 3 until firm.)
4. So put a yellow mark on one vehicle. ✔
5. Here's another coloring rule. Listen: Color all buildings green. What's the rule? (Signal.) *Color all buildings green.*
   * (Repeat step 5 until firm.)
6. So put a green mark on one building. ✔
7. There's one more thing to do. One vehicle has a missing part. What vehicle is that? (Signal.) *An airplane.* Yes, one of the airplanes.
   * What part of the airplane is missing? (Signal.) *A wing.* Yes, a wing.
   * Before you color the airplane, follow the dots and make a wing.
8. Remember—the marks show you what color to make the vehicles and the buildings. You can color the other objects any color you want.

**12**

*Side 2   Lesson 12*

**12**

*Lesson 12   Side 1*

Name _____

## Grade 2 Language Arts— Lesson 35

Lesson 35 from Grade 2 Language Arts includes material from the following components:

- Language Arts Presentation Book A
- Workbook

You begin Lesson 35 by presenting Workbook exercises on alphabetical order, map directions, and classification (exercises 1–3). During each exercise, students write and check their answers. Then you read students a story that involves ambiguous sentences (exercise 4). Finally, students interpret and rewrite ambiguous sentences in the Workbook (exercise 5).

# LESSON 35

## Objectives

- Alphabetize words that start with different letters. (Exercise 1)
- Complete descriptions involving relative directions. (Exercise 2)
- **Indicate the number of objects in larger and smaller classes.** (Exercise 3)
- Listen to part 2 of a story and answer comprehension questions. (Exercise 4)
- Edit sentences to eliminate pronoun ambiguity. (Exercise 5)

## WORKBOOK

### EXERCISE 1  Alphabetical Order

| | |
|---|---|
| helpful | knock |
| jumpy | gate |
| farmer | landed |
| inside | |

1. _____
2. _____
3. _____
4. _____
5. _____
6. _____
7. _____

1. Open your workbook to lesson 35 and find part A. ✔
- Find the words in the box. You're going to write these words in alphabetical order. First you have to find the word that is earliest in the alphabet.
  I don't see a word that begins with **A.**
  I don't see a word that begins with **B.**
  I don't see a word that begins with **C.**
  I don't see a word that begins with **D.**
- Look at the list and see if you can find one that begins with **E.** ✔
2. Did you find a word that begins with **E**? (Signal.) *No.*
- You looked for words that begin with **A, B, C, D,** and **E.** What letter will you look for next? (Signal.) *F.*
3. See if you can find a word that begins with **F.** ✔
- Everybody, did you find a word that begins with **F**? (Signal.) *Yes.*
4. Write it on line 1. Cross it out from the list. Then write the other words in alphabetical order.
  (Observe students and give feedback.)

5. (Write on the board:)

> 1. farmer
> 2. gate
> 3. helpful
> 4. inside
> 5. jumpy
> 6. knock
> 7. landed

- Here's what you should have.

### EXERCISE 2  Map Directions

**Relative Direction**

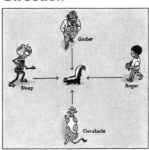

1. The skunk is north of _____
2. The skunk is east of _____
3. The skunk is west of _____
4. The skunk is south of _____

1. Find part B. You're going to look at the arrows and complete sentences.
2. Sentence 1: The skunk is north of something. You complete that sentence with the name of the object on the north arrow.
- Sentence 2: The skunk is east of something. You complete that sentence with the name of the object on the east arrow.
- Sentence 3: The skunk is west of something. You complete that sentence with the name of the object on the west arrow.

- Sentence 4: The skunk is south of something. You complete that sentence with the name of the object on the south arrow.
- Your turn: Complete all the sentences. Raise your hand when you're finished. ✔
3. Check your work. I'll read the first part of each sentence. You tell me the last part.
- Sentence 1: The skunk is north of . . . (Signal.) *Clarabelle.*
- Sentence 2: The skunk is east of . . . (Signal.) *Bleep.*
- Sentence 3: The skunk is west of . . . (Signal.) *Roger.*
- Sentence 4: The skunk is south of . . . (Signal.) *Goober.*

### EXERCISE 3 Classification

**Mental Manipulation**

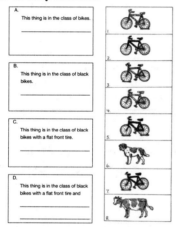

1. Everybody, find part C. ✔
   The pictures show different bikes. The sentences tell about the classes.
- I'll read the sentences. Follow along.
- Touch sentence A. ✔
  This thing is in the class of bikes. That's the big class.
- Touch sentence B. ✔
  This thing is the class of black bikes. That's a smaller class.
- Touch sentence C. ✔
  This thing is in the class of black bikes with a flat front tire.
2. Here's what you're going to do. Below each sentence, write the number of every picture that sentence tells about.

- Touch sentence A. ✔
  This thing is in the class of bikes. You have to write the number of every picture that sentence tells about. You'll write the number of every picture that shows a bike.
- Picture 1 shows a bike, so you'd write number 1 on the line below sentence A.
- Picture 2 shows a bike, so you'd write number 2 under the sentence.
- Listen: Write the number of every picture that shows a bike. Raise your hand when you're finished.
  (Observe students and give feedback.)
- (Write on the board:)

> **1, 2, 3, 4, 5, 7**

- Here are the numbers you should have under sentence A—1, 2, 3, 4, 5, 7. Raise your hand if you got it right. ✔
- Everybody, look at picture number 6.
- Why didn't you write that number under the first sentence? (Call on individual students. Idea: *A St. Bernard is not a bike.*)
- Everybody, what other number didn't you write? (Signal.) *8.*
- Why didn't you write the number for Clarabelle? (Call on a student. Idea: *She's not a bike.*)
3. Touch sentence B. ✔
   This thing is in the class of **black** bikes. Is that class bigger or smaller than the class of bikes? (Signal.) *Smaller.*
- So you should have fewer things in this class.
- Write the number of everything that's in the class of **black** bikes. Raise your hand when you're finished.
  (Observe students and give feedback.)
- (Write on the board:)

> **2, 5, 7**

- Here are the numbers you should have for the things in the class of black bikes. Raise your hand if you got it right.
4. Touch sentence C. ✔
   This thing is in the class of black bikes with a flat front tire. Remember, it's in the class of **black** bikes with a flat front tire, not just any old bike with a flat front tire. Write the numbers for the things in that class. Raise your hand when you're finished.
   (Observe students and give feedback.)

- Everybody, which things are in the class of black bikes with a flat front tire? (Signal.) *5 and 7.*
- There are two things in that class, but we're going to tell about only one thing.
- Touch **only** bike 5. ✔
  That's the bike with the flat front tire you'll tell about.

5. Touch sentence D. ✔
   It says: This thing is in the class of black bikes with a flat front tire and . . . something else.

- You're going to complete that sentence so it tells about bike 5 and **no other** bike that's black and has a flat front tire.
- Look at the picture of bike 5. See what else you can say about that bike and write it. That bike has a flat front tire and something else. Raise your hand when you're finished. (Observe students and give feedback.)
- (Call on different students to read their sentence. Praise sentences that tell about a flat rear tire. Say:) That's a really super sentence: Raise your hand if you wrote that super sentence. (Praise sentences that tell about a flat rear tire.)
- This is pretty hard, but a lot of you are too smart to get fooled.

### EXERCISE 4  Zelda the Artist *Part 2*

#### Storytelling

- I'm going to read some more about Zelda the artist. Listen:

Zelda read through Mrs. Hudson's book. Most of it was very, very boring. It told about things that were not very exciting—the rain falling in the springtime, chickens running around the barnyard, people going on long train trips—very boring.

Zelda did a couple of illustrations. The first one she did was for the part that said, "When we were on the farm, my brother and my sister had pet pigs. They just loved to roll around in the mud."

Zelda made a beautiful picture of Mrs. Hudson's brother and sister rolling around in the mud next to the barn.

In the picture that Zelda drew, the pet pigs were standing there, looking at the students in the mud. When Zelda finished that picture, she said, "That woman must have a very strange family."

Then she did the next illustration. That one was for the part that said, "Every day the children rode their horses through the valley. Their tails flew in the wind."

- Who does Zelda think had the tails? (Signal.) *The students.*
- Who was Mrs. Hudson telling about when she wrote: "**Their** tails flew in the wind"? (Signal.) *The horses.*

Zelda didn't know how many students to draw or how long to make their "tails." But at last she decided to show three children riding horses. She gave each of the children a long tail. She gave the horses regular horse tails. After she finished the illustration, she said, "That woman sure knows some very strange people."

Then she went on to the next part. It said: "We always kept a glass on top of the refrigerator. We kept it full of water."

- What does Zelda think was "full of water"? (Signal.) *The refrigerator.*
- What was really full of water? (Signal.) *The glass.*

Zelda decided to show a picture of somebody opening the refrigerator and water pouring out. She said to herself, "I don't know any other way to show that it was full of water."

Zelda didn't know what to put inside the glass. So she left the glass empty.

**180**    *Lesson 35*

The part that was marked for the next illustration said this: "Our car stopped on top of the mountain. It was out of gas."

- I think we've got another problem. Listen again:

"Our car stopped on top of the mountain. It was out of gas."

- What part is Zelda going to confuse this time? (Call on a student. Idea: *What is out of gas.*)

Zelda read that part again and again. At last she said, "How am I going to show that the mountain is out of gas? I can't illustrate this picture." Zelda called Mrs. Hudson and said, "I'm having trouble with one illustration. It's for the part that says, 'Our car stopped on top of the mountain. It was out of gas.' How am I going to show it was out of gas?"

"I see what you mean, my dear. Just looking at the picture, you wouldn't really know that it was out of gas, would you?"

"I sure wouldn't," Zelda said.

"Well, what if you sort of showed the inside of it, and we could see the gas gauge?"

"The gas gauge?"

"Yes, my dear. You could put us on top of the mountain, looking inside the window, and show the gas gauge."

"Looking inside **the window?"**

"Of course."

"It has a window?"

"Well, certainly. It has windows all the way around it."

"Wow," Zelda said. "I'll draw it, but I've never seen one with windows before."

"Well, the next time I go over to your place, I'll show you a picture of it."

Zelda said, "I'll take your word for it."

After Zelda hung up the phone, she did the illustration of a great mountain with a car parked on top. The mountain had windows all the way around, and inside one of the windows was a great huge gas gauge.

Zelda looked at the picture and said, "That woman has sure been to some strange places."

The next part of the book that was marked said this: "Our car went down the dirt road, leaving a dust cloud behind. Soon, it floated away on the breeze."

- Uh-oh. I think Zelda is going to have trouble again. Listen to that part again:

"Our car went down the dirt road, leaving a dust cloud behind. Soon, it floated away on the breeze."

- What do you think she'll get wrong this time? (Call on a student. Idea: *What floated away.*)

Zelda read the part to herself two times. Then she shook her head and made the illustration. It showed a car floating through the air over a dirt road. Zelda said to herself, "That woman sure has some strange vehicles, too."

Zelda worked on the illustrations week after week. And every week Mrs. Hudson would call Zelda and remind her that the book had to be finished soon. "Remember, Zelda," she would say, "this book must go to the publisher by March. I certainly hope you'll be done with all the illustrations by then."

- The publisher takes the story Mrs. Hudson wrote and Zelda's illustrations and makes them into a regular book that people can buy.

Every time Mrs. Hudson called to remind Zelda of getting the book ready for the publisher, Zelda would say, "I'm working as fast as I can, but some of these illustrations are not very easy."

Every week, Mrs. Hudson called and said the same thing. Every week, Zelda told her the same thing.

But then, in the middle of February, Mrs. Hudson called and started to say, "Remember, Zelda, this book must go to the publisher before . . . "

"I'm done with the illustrations," Zelda said.

"How perfectly wonderful!" Mrs. Hudson said. "How marvelous! Isn't this just grand?"

She told Zelda that she would be right over and she was. She was still talking about how wonderful everything was when she arrived at Zelda's place. "This is just perfect," she said. "I can hardly wait to see your illustrations, my dear."

Then Mrs. Hudson saw Zelda's illustrations. She looked at the first one, and her eyes got wide, and her face became very serious and stiff. Her face stayed that way as she looked at the next illustration, and the next illustration, and the next illustration. She wasn't saying anything like, "How wonderful this is." She wasn't saying **anything.** She was just staring at those illustrations with wide eyes and a very stiff face.

At last, she dropped the illustrations on the floor and said to Zelda, "What have you done to my wonderful book? These illustrations are awful. They are terrible. They are unbelievable. They are . . ." (She had run out of bad words.)

Zelda said, "Well, I did the best I could. I had never seen any of the things your book told about. Like the picture of the students with their tails flying in the wind. I didn't know if they should have monkey tails, lion tails or short little bunny tails."

"Stop it," Mrs. Hudson said. "I do not find your wit one bit funny. And I find your illustrations terrible, awful, unbelievable, and simply . . . " (She'd run out of bad words again.)

"Well," Zelda said, "I'm sorry. I don't have time to redo them now, but I could . . . "

"No, this book must be at the publisher by March. If it's not at the publisher by March, it doesn't get published."

"Well," Zelda said, "Maybe you can send it in without the illustrations."

"No," Mrs. Hudson said, "I promised the publisher that I would have twenty beautiful illustrations. I didn't know that I would have twenty illustrations that were unbelievable, terrible, awful, and just plain . . . "

So Mrs. Hudson picked up the illustrations, picked up her book and marched out of Zelda's place.

Nobody was very happy.

- Oh dear. I wonder what's going to happen. We'll have to wait till next time to find out.

## EXERCISE 5   Interpreting Ambiguous Sentences

1. My brother and my sister had pet pigs. They just loved to roll around in the mud.

2. We always kept a glass on top of the refrigerator. We kept it full of water.

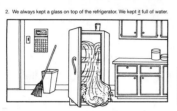

1. Everybody, find part D. ✔
   These are the illustrations that Zelda drew for two parts of the story.
   - You're going to fix up the sentences with the names that Zelda thought the sentences were talking about.

2. Touch number 1. ✔
   The picture below number 1 shows Mrs. Hudson's brother and sister rolling around in the mud.
   - I'll read what number 1 says. You follow along: My brother and my sister had pet pigs. They just loved to roll around in the mud.

- Touch the word that's underlined. ✔ Everybody, what word is underlined? (Signal.) *They.*
- What was Mrs. Hudson **really** writing about? (Signal.) *The pigs.*
- What did Zelda think she was writing about? (Signal.) *Mrs. Hudson's brother and sister.*

3. Listen: Cross out the word **they** and write **my brother and sister** above the crossed-out word. Raise your hand when you're finished.
   (Observe students and give feedback.)

4. Touch number 2. ✔
   I'll read what it says: We always kept a glass on top of the refrigerator. We kept it full of water.
- Touch the word that's underlined. ✔ Everybody, what word is underlined? (Signal.) *It.*
- What was Mrs. Hudson really writing about? (Signal.) *The glass.*
- What did Zelda think she was writing about? (Signal.) *The refrigerator.*
- Listen: Cross out the word **it** and write **the refrigerator.** Raise your hand when you're finished.
   (Observe students and give feedback.)

5. Now the sentences for both pictures tell what Zelda thought she should illustrate.
- Later you can color the pictures.

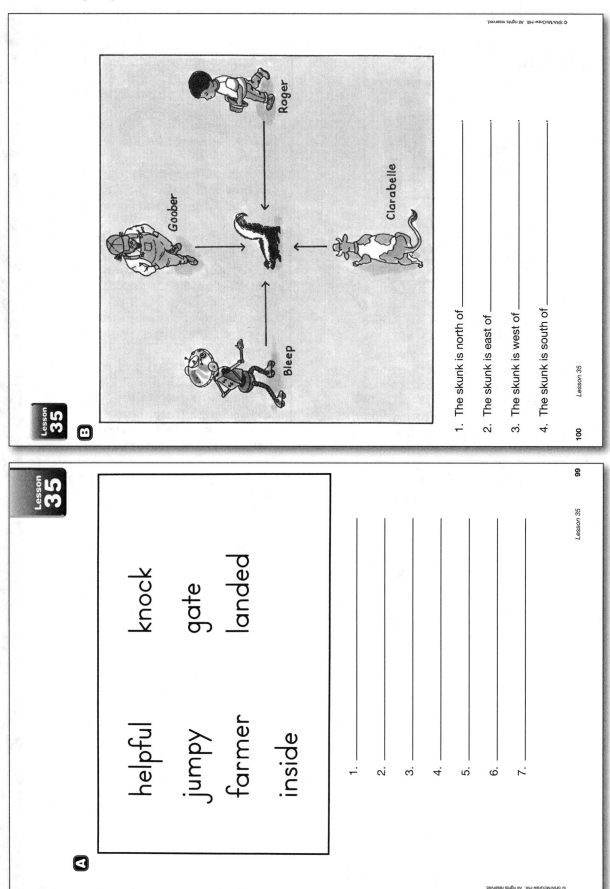

**Lesson 35**

**B**

Roger

Goober

Clarabelle

Bleep

1. The skunk is north of _____

2. The skunk is east of _____

3. The skunk is west of _____

4. The skunk is south of _____

*Lesson 35*

100

**Lesson 35**

**A**

helpful   knock

jumpy     gate

farmer    landed

inside

1. _____
2. _____
3. _____
4. _____
5. _____
6. _____
7. _____

*Lesson 35*

99

# Grade 2 Language Arts Workbook

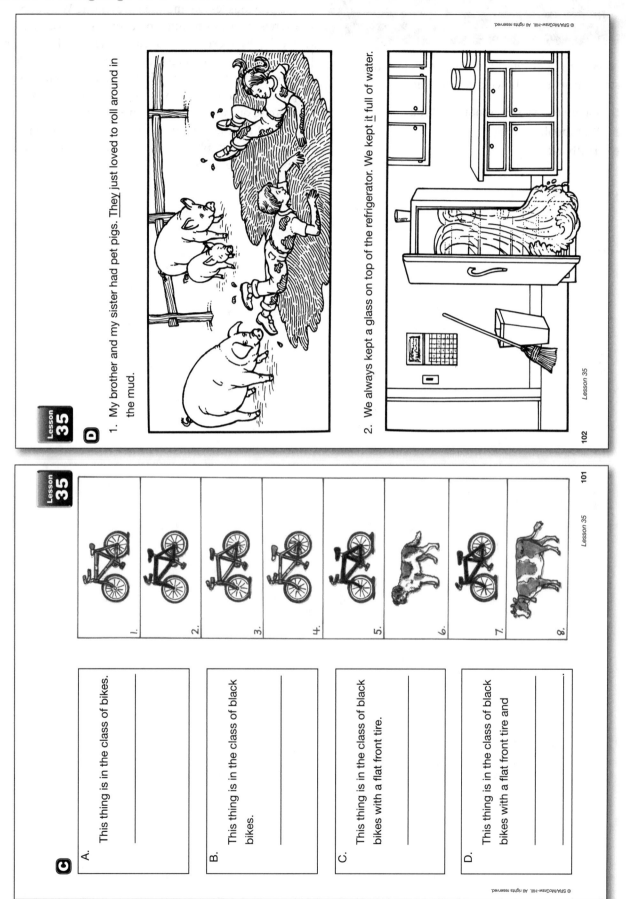

**Lesson 35**

**D**

1. My brother and my sister had pet pigs. <u>They</u> just loved to roll around in the mud.

2. We always kept a glass on top of the refrigerator. We kept <u>it</u> full of water.

**Lesson 35**

1. 2. 3. 4. 5. 6. 7. 8.

**C**

A. This thing is in the class of bikes.
_____

B. This thing is in the class of black bikes.
_____

C. This thing is in the class of black bikes with a flat front tire.
_____

D. This thing is in the class of black bikes with a flat front tire and
_____

## Grade 3 Language Arts— Lesson 17

Lesson 17 from Grade 3 Language Arts includes material from the following components:

- Language Arts Presentation Book
- Workbook
- Textbook

You begin Lesson 17 by returning student work from the previous lesson and then presenting Workbook exercises on editing and possessives (exercises 1–3). During each exercise, students write and check their answers. Then you present a writing activity in which students write a paragraph that describes a missing picture (exercise 4). Next you present a Textbook exercise on two-word verbs (exercise 5). Finally, you present another writing activity in which students write a paragraph that describes a series of pictures (exercises 6 and 7).

## LESSON 17

### Objectives

- Discriminate between run-on sentences and sentences that name two actions. (Exercise 2)
- Construct sentences with possessive words. (Exercise 3)
- **Write a paragraph that infers what must have happened in a missing picture.** (Exercise 4)
- **Identify the verbs in sentences that have 1-word verbs and in sentences that have 2-word verbs.** (Exercise 5)
- Say sentences that report on the important events in each picture in an action sequence of pictures. (Exercise 6)
- Construct a paragraph that reports on an action sequence of pictures. (Exercise 7)

### WORKBOOK

#### EXERCISE 1  Feedback on Lesson 16

- (Before handing back student's work from lesson 16, read one or two well-written paragraphs that meet all the checks.)
- (Hand back students' work from lesson 16.)
- Praise students
  a. who had correct answers for all items in lesson 16 skill exercises, and
  b. whose edited paragraph meets all the checks.
- Provide feedback on any exercises that were troublesome.

#### EXERCISE 2  Editing

#### Run-On Sentences

1. Everybody, open your workbook to lesson 17 and find part A. ✔
- Not all sentences that have the word **and** are run-ons. Remember the rule: Run-ons have more than one subject, so you can make more than one sentence out of the words. If you can't make more than one sentence out of the words, it's not a run-on.
2. Item 1: Melissa fed her dog and she went inside to change her shoes. Circle **Melissa.** Then see if the item has another subject. Raise your hand when you know.
- Everybody, does that item have more than one subject? (Signal.) *Yes.*
- So it's a run-on. Fix it up. Raise your hand when you're finished.

- Check your work. Everybody, read the first sentence in item 1. (Signal.) *Melissa fed her dog.*
- Read the second sentence in item 1. (Signal.) *She went inside to change her shoes.*
3. Item 2: Ann loved horses and her big brother wanted a horse for his birthday. Circle **Ann.** Then see if the item has another subject. Raise your hand when you know.
- Everybody, does that item have more than one subject? (Signal.) *Yes.*
- So it's a run-on. Fix it up.
- Check your work. Everybody, read the first sentence in item 2. (Signal.) *Ann loved horses.*
- Read the second sentence in item 2. (Signal.) *Her big brother wanted a horse for his birthday.*
4. Item 3: The children went to the farm and played with the animals. Circle **the children.** Then see if the item has another subject. Raise your hand when you know.
- Everybody, does that item have more than one subject? (Signal.) *No.*
- So it's not a run-on. What's the subject of that sentence? (Signal.) *The children.*
- What's the predicate? (Signal.) *Went to the farm and played with the animals.*

5. Your turn: Fix up the rest of the items in part A. Circle the first subject. Then see if there is another subject. If there is another subject, the item is a run-on. Fix it up. If there is only one subject, the item is not a run-on. It's just a sentence that tells about two things somebody did. Pencils down when you're finished.
(Observe students and give feedback.)

6. Check your work.
• Item 4: My brother swept the floor and washed the dishes. What did you circle? (Signal.) *My brother.*
• Is item 4 a run-on? (Signal.) *No.*
• Item 5: A man and a woman watched TV and he had a sore arm. What did you circle? (Signal.) *A man and a woman.*
• Is item 5 a run-on? (Signal.) *Yes.*
• Read the first fixed-up sentence. (Signal.) *A man and a woman watched TV.*
• Read the second fixed-up sentence. (Signal.) *He had a sore arm.*
• Item 6: Ron went to the park and fed the birds. What did you circle? (Signal.) *Ron.*
• Is item 6 a run-on? (Signal.) *No.*

7. Raise your hand if you fixed up all the run-ons. Great job.
• Everybody else, fix up any mistakes you made in part A.

### EXERCISE 3   Possessive

**Apostrophe + S**

1. Everybody, pencils down. Find part B. ✔
• You're going to complete sentences that tell about something that belongs to something else.

2. Touch item 1.
The pencil belonged to a girl. The pencil was yellow. Listen to the first sentence again: The pencil belonged to **a girl.** Who did the pencil belong to? (Signal.) *A girl.*
• So what do we write for the pencil belonged to a girl? (Signal.) *A girl's pencil.*
• Spell **girl's.** (Signal.) *G-i-r-l-apostrophe-s.*

3. Touch item 2.
The nest belonged to that bird. The nest had eggs in it. Who did that nest belong to? (Signal.) *That bird.*
• So what do we write **for the nest belonged to that bird?** (Signal.) *That bird's nest.*

• Spell **bird's.** (Signal.) *B-i-r-d-apostrophe-s.*

4. Touch item 3.
The glasses belonged to my friend. The glasses were broken. Who did the glasses belong to? (Signal.) *My friend.*
• So what do we write? (Signal.) *My friend's glasses.*

5. Complete the items in part B. Just rewrite the first sentence for each item and you'll complete the new sentence. Pencils down when you're finished.
(Observe students and give feedback.)

6. Let's check your work.
• Item 1: The pencil belonged to a girl. The pencil was yellow. Read the sentence you completed. (Signal.) *A girl's pencil was yellow.*
• Item 2: The nest belonged to that bird. The nest had eggs in it. Read the sentence you completed. (Signal.) *That bird's nest had eggs in it.*
• Item 3: The glasses belonged to my friend. The glasses were broken. Read the sentence you completed. (Signal.) *My friend's glasses were broken.*
• Item 4: The bottle belonged to her baby. The bottle had milk in it. Read the sentence you completed. (Signal.) *Her baby's bottle had milk in it.*

7. Raise your hand if you made no mistakes. Great job.
• Everybody else, fix up any mistakes you made in part B.

### LINED PAPER • TEXTBOOK

### EXERCISE 4   Inference

**Missing Picture**

1. Everybody, take out a sheet of lined paper and write your name and lesson 17 on the top line. Pencils down when you're finished. ✔
• Find part C in your workbook.
• You've **reported** on what pictures show, but you can't always report. Sometimes you have to be smart and figure out what must have happened. The pictures in part C are supposed to show what happened first and next and next, but the middle picture is missing.

2. Let's see if you can figure out what must have happened in the middle picture by comparing picture 1 and picture 3. Touch the candle in picture 1. Who can tell about the candle in picture 1? (Call on a student. Idea: *The candle is falling from the shelf.*)

- Touch the candle in picture 3. Where is the candle in picture 3? (Call on a student. Idea: *The candle is on the newspapers.*)

- Touch the newspapers in picture 1 and in picture 3. What is different about the newspapers in picture 1 and picture 3? (Call on a student: *In picture 3, the newspapers are burning.*)

- Why did the newspapers start to burn? (Call on a student. Idea: *The burning candle fell on the newspapers.*)

- Touch the bucket in picture 1 and in picture 3. What is different about the bucket in picture 1 and picture 3? (Call on a student. Idea: *In picture 1, the bucket is on the floor. In picture 3, the woman is holding the bucket.*)

- What did the woman do in the middle picture? (Call on a student. Idea: *The woman picked up a bucket.*)

3. Here's the first part of the story: A woman was looking out the window. Her cat jumped onto a shelf. The cat knocked over a burning candle that was on the shelf.

4. Now, you'll tell me what must have happened in the middle picture. You'll tell about the candle, the newspapers and the woman.

- Raise your hand when you can say a sentence that tells what the candle must have done in the missing picture. (Call on several students. Praise sentences such as: *The candle fell on a pile of newspapers.* For each good sentence: Everybody, say that sentence.)

5. Raise your hand when you can say a sentence that tells what the newspapers must have done in the missing picture. (Call on several students. Praise sentences such as: *The newspapers started to burn.* For each good sentence: Everybody, say that sentence.)

6. Now make up a sentence that tells what the woman must have done in the middle picture. Be careful. Don't tell what she did in the last picture. Tell what she must have done in the middle picture. (Call on several students. Praise sentences such as: *The woman picked up a bucket of water.* For each good sentence: Everybody, say that sentence.)

7. I'll read a paragraph that tells what happened in the missing picture: The candle fell onto a pile of newspapers on the floor. The newspapers started to burn. The woman picked up a bucket of water.

8. I'll say those sentences again.

- The candle fell onto a pile of newspapers on the floor. Say that sentence. (Signal.) *The candle fell onto a pile of newspapers.*

- The newspapers started to burn. Say that sentence. (Signal.) *The newspapers started to burn.*

- The woman picked up a bucket of water. Say that sentence. (Signal.) *The woman picked up a bucket of water.*

9. I'll read the words in the vocabulary box: **bucket, fell, burn.**

10. Your turn: Write a paragraph. Write sentences that tell what must have happened in the middle picture. Tell about the candle, the newspapers and the woman. Pencils down when you're finished. (Observe students and give feedback.)

11. I'll call on different students to read their paragraph.

- (Call on several students. Praise sentences such as: *The candle landed on the newspapers. The newspapers started to burn. The woman picked up a bucket of water.*)

12. Let's see if you did a good job of giving a clear picture of what must have happened in the middle picture. Open your textbook to lesson 17 and find part C. ✔
- It shows the middle picture. Look at the candle in that picture. (Call on a student:) Where is it? *On the newspapers.*
- (Call on a student:) What started burning in that picture? The newspapers.
- (Call on a student:) What did the woman do? (Idea: *She picked up a bucket of water.*)
13. Raise your hand if your paragraph gave a clear picture of what must have happened in the middle picture.
- You are really good at figuring things out.

**EXERCISE 5   Two-word Verbs**

1. Skip a line on your paper. Then number your paper 1 through 6. Pencils down when you're finished. ✔
- Find part D in your textbook.
- Some of the sentences have a one-word verb and some of the sentences have a two-word verb. Remember, the verb comes right after the subject.
2. Sentence 1: The boys rode their bikes. What's the subject? (Signal.) *The boys.*
- Listen: What's the verb? (Signal.) *Rode.*
- Sentence 2: Her mother was singing to herself. What's the subject? (Signal.) *Her mother.*
- What's the verb? (Signal.) *Was singing.*
- Sentence 3: I slipped on the ice. What's the subject? (Signal.) *I.*
- What's the verb? (Signal.) *Slipped.*
- Sentence 4: She was eating in her room. What's the subject? (Signal.) *She.*
- What's the verb? (Signal.) *Was eating.*
- Sentence 5: They sat on a bench. What's the subject? (Signal.) *They.*
- What's the verb? (Signal.) *Sat.*
- (Repeat step 2 until firm.)
3. Your turn: Write the **verb** for each sentence. If the verb has two words, write both words. Pencils down when you're finished.
   (Observe students and give feedback.)

4. Check your work.
- Sentence 1: The boys rode their bikes. What's the verb? (Signal.) *Rode.*
- Sentence 2: Her mother was singing to herself. What's the verb? (Signal.) *Was singing.*
- Sentence 3: I slipped on the ice. What's the verb? (Signal.) *Slipped.*
- Sentence 4: She was eating in her room. What's the verb? (Signal.) *Was eating.*
- Sentence 5: They sat on a bench. What's the verb? (Signal.) *Sat.*
- Sentence 6: My brother and sister played in the park. What's the verb? (Signal.) *Played.*
5. Raise your hand if you made no mistakes. Great job.
- Everybody else, fix up any mistakes you made in part D.

**EXERCISE 6   Preparing to Write a Paragraph**

1. Everybody, pencils down.
   Find part E in your textbook.
   I'll read the instructions: Write a paragraph that reports on what happened.
   The persons and things in these pictures are not numbered. Before you write, we'll say sentences that report on the important things that happened.

2. Everybody, touch picture 1.
* Raise your hand when you can say a sentence that reports on the main thing the gorilla did in that picture. (Call on several students. Praise sentences such as: *A gorilla walked out of its cage.* For each good sentence: Everybody, say that sentence.)
3. Everybody, touch picture 2.
* Several important things happened in that picture. Raise your hand when you can say a sentence that reports on what the zookeeper did in that picture. (Call on several students. Praise sentences such as: *The zookeeper made a trail of bananas that led to the cage.* For each good sentence: Everybody, say that sentence.)
* Raise your hand when you can say a sentence that reports on the main thing the gorilla did in that picture. (Call on several students. Praise sentences such as: *The gorilla picked up the bananas and walked towards the cage.* For each good sentence: Everybody, say that sentence.)
4. Everybody, touch picture 3.
* Raise your hand when you can say a sentence that reports on the main thing the gorilla did in that picture. (Call on several students. Praise sentences such as: *The gorilla walked into the cage.* For each good sentence: Everybody, say that sentence.)
* Raise your hand when you can say a sentence that reports on the main thing the zookeeper did in that picture. (Call on several students. Praise sentences such as: *The zookeeper closed the gate behind the gorilla.* For each good sentence: Everybody, say that sentence.)
5. I'll read a passage that reports on what happened: A gorilla escaped from its cage. The zookeeper made a trail of bananas that led to the cage. The gorilla picked up the bananas. The gorilla walked into the cage. The zookeeper closed the gate behind the gorilla.

## EXERCISE 7   Writing a Paragraph—No Numbers

1. You're going to write a paragraph that reports on what happened in these pictures.
2. Touch the words in the vocabulary box as I read them: **gorilla, walked, bananas, trail, cage, picked, escaped, followed, zookeeper.** Be sure to spell those words correctly if you use them in your paragraph.
3. After your write your paragraph, you'll check it. Remember the new checks:
* Check 1 says: Did you give a clear picture of what happened? That means that you have a sentence for each important thing that happened, and the sentences are written to give a clear picture of what happened.
* Check 2 says: Did you fix up any run-on sentences? That means there are no run-on sentences in your paragraph.
4. Write your paragraph. For each picture, write sentences that report on the important things that happened. Name a person or thing, then tell what the person or thing did. You can use the sentences we just said or you can use other sentences. You have 8 minutes. (Observe students and give feedback.)
5. (After 8 minutes, say: ) Stop writing. You'll check what you have written so far. Make 4 check boxes under your paragraph.
Check 1 says: Did you give a clear picture of what happened? Read your paragraph carefully. If you left out an important sentence, write it below your paragraph and make an arrow to show where that sentence should go. Read over your paragraph for check 1. When you are sure it gives a clear picture, put a check in box 1. (Observe students and give feedback.)
6. Check 2 says: Did you fix up any run-on sentences? Read your paragraph over again. Fix up any run-on sentences. When you're sure there are no run-on sentences, put a check in box 2. (Observe students and give feedback.)

**86**    *Lesson 17*

7. Read your paragraph over for check 3 and fix up any problems. When you're sure that every sentence begins with a capital and ends with a period, put a check in the third box. (Observe students and give feedback.)

- Read your paragraph over for check 4 and fix up any problems. When you're sure that each sentence tells what somebody did, make a check in the fourth box. (Observe students and give feedback.)

8. I'll read over your paragraphs before the next lesson. For any problems with a check, I'll write letters in the margin.

- What letters will I write if your paragraph does not give a clear picture of what happened? (Signal.) *WH.*
- What letters will I write if your paragraph has a run-on sentence? (Signal.) *RO.*
- What letters will I write if a sentence does not begin with a capital or end with a period? (Signal.) *CP.*

- What letters will I write if a sentence does not tell what somebody did? (Signal.) *D-I-D.*
- During the next lesson, you'll fix up any errors. I'll have several students who did not have any problems with checks read their paragraph.

---

*Note:*

- Collect the students' workbooks and lined papers.
- Check the skill exercises in the workbook and on the lined paper. Mark any items that were not corrected. Where appropriate, write brief comments.
- Check the students' paragraphs.
  Write letters in the margin for any sentence that does not satisfy a check. See the *Language Atrs Teacher's Guide* for information on how to respond to other problems, such as spelling and grammar errors.

---

# Grade 3 Language Arts Workbook

**C** Write sentences that tell what must have happened in the middle picture. Tell about **the candle, the newspapers** and **the woman.**

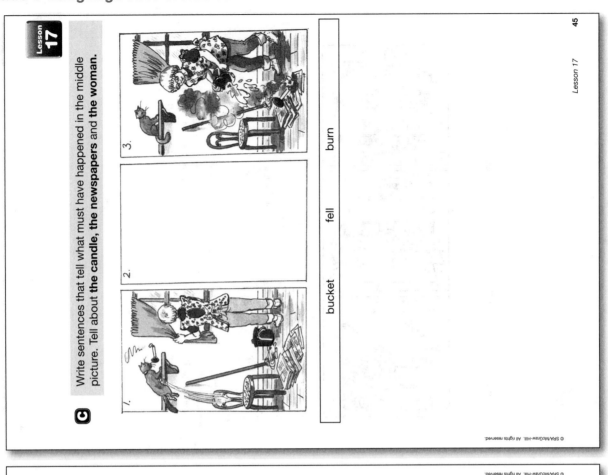

2.

3.

| bucket | fell | burn |
|--------|------|------|

---

**A** Fix up the run-on sentences.

1. Melissa fed her dog and she went inside to change her shoes.

2. Ann loved horses and her big brother wanted a horse for his birthday.

3. The children went to the farm and played with the animals.

4. My brother swept the floor and washed the dishes.

5. A man and a woman watched TV and he had a sore arm.

6. Ron went to the park and fed the birds.

**B** Rewrite each item with an apostrophe **s.**

1. The pencil belonged to **a girl.** The pencil was yellow.

   _____ was yellow.

2. The nest belonged to **that bird.** The nest had eggs in it.

   _____ had eggs in it.

3. The glasses belonged to **my friend.** The glasses were broken.

   _____ were broken.

4. The bottle belonged to **her baby.** The bottle had milk in it.

   _____ had milk in it.

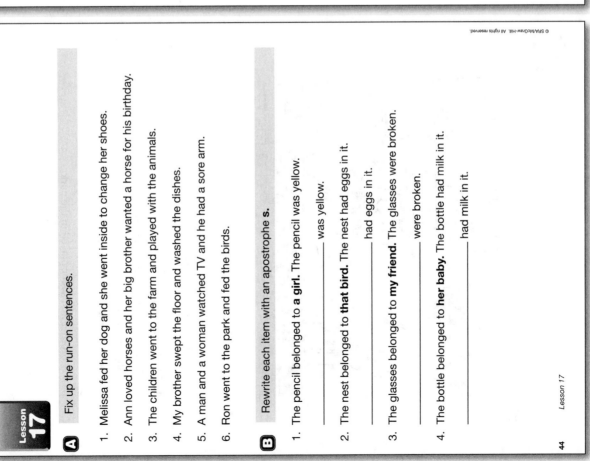

**Lesson 17**

**E**

Write a paragraph that reports on what happened.

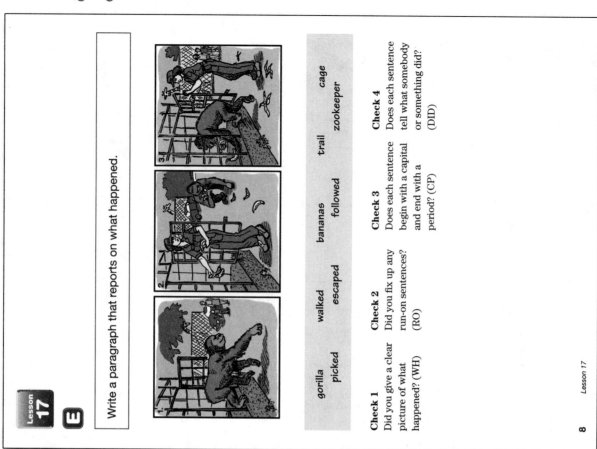

gorilla    walked    bananas    trail    cage

picked    escaped    followed    zookeeper

**Check 1**
Did you give a clear picture of what happened? (WH)

**Check 2**
Did you fix up any run-on sentences? (RO)

**Check 3**
Does each sentence begin with a capital and end with a period? (CP)

**Check 4**
Does each sentence tell what somebody or something did? (DID)

8    Lesson 17

**Lesson 17**

**C**

**D**

Write the verb for each sentence.

1. The boys rode their bikes.
2. Her mother was singing to herself.
3. I slipped on the ice.
4. She was eating in her room.
5. They sat on a bench.
6. My brother and sister played in the park.

Lesson 17    7

# Grade 4 Language Arts—Lesson 26

Lesson 26 from Grade 4 Language Arts includes material from the following components:

- Language Arts Presentation Book
- Textbook

All the exercises in the Language Arts Presentation Book for Lesson 26 relate to the Textbook, and the procedure for each exercise is similar. First you explain the Textbook exercise. Then students write their answers on lined paper. Finally, students check their answers as a group.

In Lesson 26, students complete seven Textbook exercises under your supervision (exercises 1–7). Topics include clarity, misleading claims, deductions, sentence writing, writing directions, false dilemmas, and following directions. Students complete the final exercise independently (exercise 8—independent work).

## LESSON 26

### Objectives

- Use facts to rewrite a general sentence so it is specific. (Exercise 1)
- Use facts to rewrite claims so they have numbers and are therefore not misleading. (Exercise 2)
- Use 2 sentences of a deduction to figure out the third sentence. (Exercise 3)
- Follow the format of a 2-sentence X-box to indicate problems with the directions for making figures. (Exercise 4)
- Write general directions that would permit one to construct any of 3 figures and specific directions that would allow one to construct only 1 of the 3 figures. (Exercise 5)
- Refer to a false dilemma and write a sentence that tells about another possibility. (Exercise 6)
- Construct figures by following clear directions. (Exercise 7)

---

### TEXTBOOK • LINED PAPER

#### EXERCISE 1  Clarity

**Writing Specific Sentences**

1. Open your textbook to lesson 26 and find part A.
   Each item has a general sentence and facts. You're going to write a specific sentence for each item. That sentence will be very clear.
2. Item 1. Read the sentence and the facts. Write the sentence that is very clear. Pencils down when you're finished.
   (Observe students and give feedback.)
- Here's what you should have: The trend in sales pleased the owners of Downtown Motors. Raise your hand if you got it right.
3. Item 2. Read the sentence and the facts. Write the sentence that is very clear. Pencils down when you're finished.
   (Observe students and give feedback.)
- Here's a good sentence: The number of traffic accidents increased after a dense fog came in. Raise your hand if you got that sentence.
4. Item 3. Read the sentence and the facts. Write the sentence that is very clear. Pencils down when you're finished.
   (Observe students and give feedback.)
- Here's what you should have: Our teacher requested information about the fire on Fifth Street. Raise your hand if you got it right.

#### EXERCISE 2  Misleading Claims

1. Find part B.
   Each sentence gives the wrong impression because it doesn't have a number that tells how many. The facts don't give the numbers, but they give you information that you can use to figure out the number.
2. Sentence 1: Z bikes weigh less than Swifto bikes. That sentence gives the impression that Z bikes weigh a lot less. You can use the numbers in the facts to figure out how much less Z bikes weigh. Raise your hand when you know how much less. ✔
- Everybody, how much less? (Signal.) *Four ounces.*
- Four ounces isn't even half a pound. Rewrite sentence 1 so it gives the number. Pencils down when you're finished.
   (Observe students and give feedback.)
- Here's the sentence you should have: Z bikes weigh four ounces less than Swifto bikes. That sentence does not give the wrong impression.
3. Sentence 2: New Bumpo cars go faster than last year's Bumpos. That sentence gives the impression that new Bumpos go a lot faster.
- Read the facts and figure out how much faster the new Bumpos are. Then rewrite the sentence so it does not give the wrong impression. Pencils down when you're finished.
   (Observe students and give feedback.)

- Here's the sentence you should have: New Bumpo cars go three miles per hour faster than last year's Bumpos. Raise your hand if you wrote that sentence.

4. Sentence 3: More people buy Blow Big gum than Big Dent gum. That sentence gives the impression that many more people buy Blow Big gum than Big Dent gum.

- Read the facts and figure out how many more people buy Blow Big gum. Then rewrite the sentence so it does not give the wrong impression. Start with the word **ten.** Pencils down when you're finished. (Observe students and give feedback.)

- Here's the sentence you should have: Ten more people buy Blow Big gum than Big Dent gum.

## EXERCISE 3  Deductions

### Missing Evidence

1. Find part C.
   A piece of evidence is missing in each deduction.

- You can make up the missing rule by combining the circled part of the conclusion with the last part of the evidence shown.

2. Deduction 1: Bees are stinging insects. Therefore, children shouldn't tease bees.

- Write the missing rule. Pencils down when you're finished.
  (Observe students and give feedback.)

- Here's what you should have: Children shouldn't tease stinging insects. Raise your hand if you got it right.

3. Everybody, say the whole deduction starting with the rule. (Signal.) *Children shouldn't tease stinging insects. Bees are stinging insects. Therefore, children shouldn't tease bees.*

- (Repeat step 3 until firm.)

4. Deduction 2: Gruppo candy is a food that contains too much sugar. Therefore, you shouldn't eat Gruppo candy.

- Write the missing rule. Pencils down when you are finished.
  (Observe students and give feedback.)

- Here's what you should have: You shouldn't eat food that contains too much sugar. Raise your hand if you got it right.

5. Say the whole deduction starting with the missing rule. (Signal.) *You shouldn't eat food that contains too much sugar. Gruppo candy is a food that contains too much sugar. Therefore, you shouldn't eat Gruppo candy.*

- (Repeat step 5 until firm.)

## EXERCISE 4  Sentence Writing

### X Box

1. Find part D.
   You're going to write two sentences for each direction. Your first sentence will tell whether the direction is inaccurate or too general. Your second sentence will tell about the figure you should make.

2. Your turn: Write both sentences for direction 1. Remember to follow the X-box rules. Pencils down when you're finished. (Observe students and give feedback.)

- Here are good sentences for direction 1: Direction 1 states that you should make a line one inch long, but that direction is too general. You should make a vertical line one inch long.

- (Call on several students to read both their sentences. Praise sentences that are precise and follow the X-box format. Correct any sentences that are vague or inaccurate.)

3. For the second item, you'll write sentences that have the words **upside-down** with a hyphen between them.

- Your turn: Write both sentences for direction 2. Pencils down when you're finished.
  (Observe students and give feedback.)

- Here are good sentences for direction 2: Direction 2 states that you should make an upside-down T one inch high, but that direction is inaccurate. You should make an upside-down A one inch high.

- (Call on several students to read both their sentences. Praise good sentences. Correct any sentences that are vague or inaccurate.)

4. Your turn: Write both sentences for direction 3. Pencils down when you're finished.
   (Observe students and give feedback.)

- (Call on several students to read both their sentences. Praise good sentences: *Direction 3 states that you should make a horizontal line one inch long, but that direction is inaccurate. You should make a vertical line one inch long.* Correct any sentences that are vague or inaccurate.)

### EXERCISE 5   Writing Directions
#### General and Specific

1. Find part E.
   There are three figures in part E. You're going to write general directions for the figures. Remember, general directions tell someone how to make any of the figures in the item.
- You figure out general directions by telling about the things that are the same about all of the figures.
2. Write the general directions for the figures on your lined paper. Pencils down when you're finished.
   (Observe students and give feedback.)
3. Here are good general directions: Make a vertical line. Write a capital letter just above the line. Write a number just below the line.
- (Call on several students to read their general directions. Praise directions that tell about all of the figures.)
4. Now you're going to write specific directions that tell how to make the first figure, just the first figure. Write specific directions for the first figure. Pencils down when you're finished.
   (Observe students and give feedback.)
5. Check your work.
- Here are good specific directions for the first figure: Make a vertical line one inch long. Write capital R just above the line. Write 2 just below the line.
- (Call on several students to read their specific directions for the first figure. Praise directions that tell only about the first figure.)
6. Raise your hand if you got both directions right. Great job.

### EXERCISE 6   False Dilemma

1. Find part F.
   Lefty is making silly statements. Liz is correcting him. You're going to write sentences that Liz might write. But be careful. Remember, you must have the word **that** in your sentence.
2. Your turn: Write your sentences for part F. Pencils down when you're finished with item 1 and item 2.
   (Observe students and give feedback.)
3. Check your work.
- Item 1. Lefty is saying, "Alice always gets A's on her report card. She must be a relative of the teacher." Liz is saying, "Another possibility is . . ."
   (Call on several students to read their sentence. Praise sentences that start with *Another possibility is that . . .* and express a reasonable idea such as: *Alice is smart; she works hard; she studies a lot.*)
4. Item 2: Lefty is saying, "Jane walked up the stairs. She must be afraid of elevators." Liz is saying, "Another possibility is . . ."
- (Call on several students to read their sentence. Praise sentences that start with *Another possibility is that . . .* and express a reasonable idea such as: *she likes to walk up stairs; the elevator is broken.*)

### EXERCISE 7   Following Directions
#### Making Figures

1. Find part G.
   The directions are clear.
- You're going to make the figure for item 1. Read the directions carefully. Make sure the lines on your figure are about the right length. Pencils down when you're finished.
   (Observe students and give feedback.)
- (Draw on the board:)

- Here's what you should have for item 1. Raise your hand if your figure looks like the figure on the board.

2. Make figure 2. Pencils down when you're finished.
   (Observe students and give feedback.)
- (Draw on the board:)

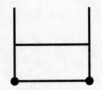

- Here's what you should have for figure 2. Raise your hand if your figure looks like the figure on the board.

**EXERCISE 8   Independent Work**

- Find part H.
  You'll do part H on your own.

# Grade 4 Language Arts Textbook

**C** Write the missing rule in each deduction.

**Deduction 1:**

Bees are stinging insects.

Therefore, (children shouldn't tease) bees.

**Deduction 2:**

Gruppo candy is a food that contains too much sugar.

Therefore, (you shouldn't eat) Gruppo candy.

**D** Follow the X-box rules and tell whether each direction is **too general** or **inaccurate**. Then tell what kind of figure you should make.

Direction ____ states that you should ____ but that direction is ____ You should make ____

| Direction | Figure |
| --- | --- |
| 1. Make a line one inch long. | |
| 2. Make an upside-down **T** one inch high. | |
| 3. Make a horizontal line one inch long. | |

---

**A** Write a specific sentence for each item.

| Sentence | Facts |
| --- | --- |
| 1. **It pleased them.** | They were the owners of Downtown Motors. |
| | It was the trend in sales. |
| [What] **pleased** [who]. | |
| 2. **They increased after it came in.** | The number of traffic accidents increased. |
| | The thing that came in was a dense fog. |
| [What] **increased after** [when]. | |
| 3. **She requested it.** | It was information about the fire on Fifth Street. |
| | She was our teacher. |
| [Who] **requested** [what]. | |

**B** Rewrite each sentence so it is not misleading.

| Sentence | Fact |
| --- | --- |
| 1. Z bikes weigh less than Swifto bikes. | Weight of bikes: Swiftos – 28 pounds 10 ounces / Z bikes – 28 pounds 6 ounces |
| 2. New Bumpo cars go faster than last year's Bumpos. | Speed of cars: New Bumpos – 83 miles per hour / Old Bumpos – 80 miles per hour |
| 3. More people buy Blow Big gum than Big Dent gum. | Number of people who buy: Blow Big gum – 2950 people / Big Dent gum – 2940 people |

# Grade 4 Language Arts Textbook

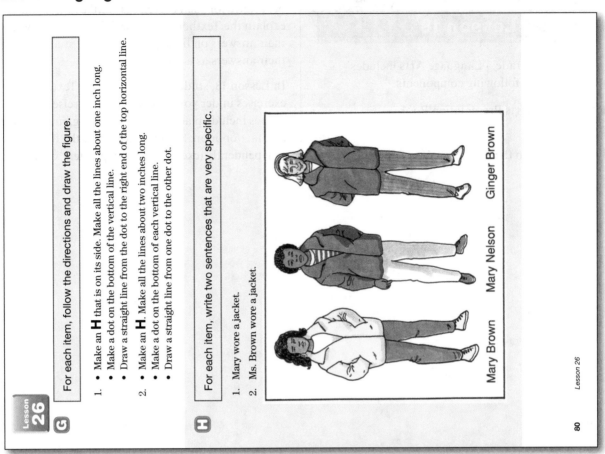

**Lesson 26**

**G** For each item, follow the directions and draw the figure.

1. • Make an **H** that is on its side. Make all the lines about one inch long.
   • Make a dot on the bottom of the vertical line.
   • Draw a straight line from the dot to the right end of the top horizontal line.

2. • Make an **H**. Make all the lines about two inches long.
   • Make a dot on the bottom of each vertical line.
   • Draw a straight line from one dot to the other dot.

**H** For each item, write two sentences that are very specific.

1. Mary wore a jacket.
2. Ms. Brown wore a jacket.

Mary Brown    Mary Nelson    Ginger Brown

*Lesson 26*    80

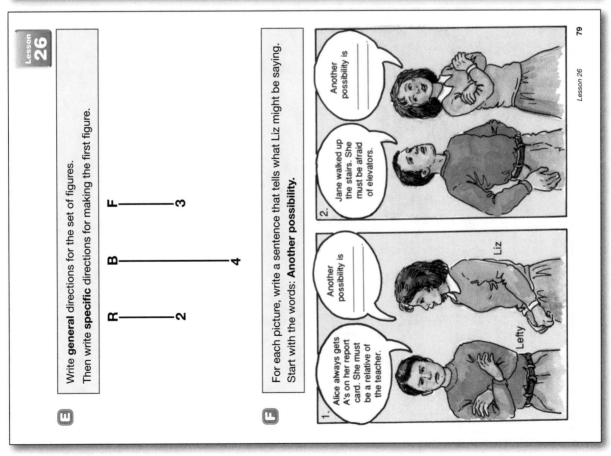

**Lesson 26**

**E** Write **general** directions for the set of figures.
Then write **specific** directions for making the first figure.

R
B
F

2
4
3

**F** For each picture, write a sentence that tells what Liz might be saying.
Start with the words: **Another possibility.**

1. Alice always gets A's on her report card. She must be a relative of the teacher.
   Another possibility is _____
   Lefty    Liz

2. Jane walked up the stairs. She must be afraid of elevators.
   Another possibility is _____

*Lesson 26*    79

## Grade 5 Language Arts— Lesson 18

Lesson 18 from Grade 5 Language Arts includes material from the following components:

- Language Arts Presentation Book
- Textbook

All the exercises in the Language Arts Presentation Book for Lesson 18 relate to the Textbook, and the procedure for each exercise is similar. First you explain the Textbook exercise. Then students write their answers on lined paper. Finally, students check their answers as a group.

In Lesson 18, students complete four Textbook exercises under your supervision (exercises 1–4). Topics include placing *only,* critiquing, unclear words, and fact/opinion. Students complete the final exercise independently (exercise 5—independent work).

# LESSON 18

## Objectives

- Write parallel sentences that include the world **only** in the appropriate position. (Exercise 1)
- Use a passage as a source for writing X-box and equal-box critiques. (Exercise 2)
- Rewrite sentences with ambiguous pronouns. (Exercise 3)
- **Distinguish statements of fact from statements of opinion.** (Exercise 4)

### TEXTBOOK • LINED PAPER

#### EXERCISE 1   Placing *Only*

1. Open your book to lesson 18 and find part A.
- You're going to learn where to put the word **only** in sentences. Each item in part A shows two sentences. The second sentence in each item disagrees with the first sentence because **it tells about fewer things.** You'll figure out where to put the word **only** in the second sentence.
2. Item 1. The first sentence says, <u>Girls *and* boys</u> <u>played</u> <u>at the picnic.</u>
- The second sentence says, **Girls played at the picnic.**
- The parts of the first sentence are underlined. The second sentence does not agree with one of these parts.
- Does the second sentence agree with the part that says **girls and boys?** (Signal.) *No.*
- Does the second sentence agree with the part that says **played?** (Signal.) *Yes.*
- Does the second sentence agree with the part that says **at the picnic?** (Signal.) *Yes.*
- Everybody, say the part of the first sentence the second sentence disagrees with. (Signal.) *Girls and boys.*
- What does the second sentence say instead of **girls and boys?** (Signal.) *Girls.*
- The word **only** goes in front of the word **girls** in the second sentence.
3. Say the second sentence with the word **only.** (Signal.) *Only girls played at the picnic.*
- (Repeat step 3 until firm.)
4. Item 2. The first sentence says, <u>Girls</u> <u>played at the picnic and in the cabin.</u>
- The second sentence says, **Girls played at the picnic.**

- The second sentence disagrees with part of the first sentence.
- Say the part of the first sentence it disagrees with. (Signal.) *At the picnic and in the cabin.*
- What does the second sentence say instead of **at the picnic and in the cabin?** (Signal.) *At the picnic.*
- So the word **only** goes just in front of the words **at the picnic.**
5. I'll say the first sentence. You say the second sentence with the word **only.**
- My turn: **Girls played at the picnic and in the cabin.** Your turn. (Signal.) *Girls played only at the picnic.*
- (Repeat step 5 until firm.)
6. Item 3. The first sentence says, <u>Girls</u> <u>played **and** talked at the picnic.</u>
- The second sentence says, **Girls played at the picnic.**
- Say the part of the first sentence that the second sentence disagrees with. (Signal.) *Played and talked.*
- What does the second sentence say instead of **played and talked?** (Signal.) *Played.*
- So the word **only** goes in front of the word **played.**
7. I'll say the first sentence. You say the second sentence with the word **only.**
- My turn: Girls played and talked at the picnic. Your turn. (Signal.) *Girls only played at the picnic.*
- (Repeat step 7 until firm.)
8. Remember, find the part of the first sentence the second sentence disagrees with. Figure out what the second sentence says instead of that part. Write the word **only** in front of those words in the second sentence.

9. Your turn: Write the second sentence in each item so it begins with the word **no** and a comma. Put the word **only** in the correct place. Don't copy the first sentence. Just write the second sentence with **no** and **only**. Put your pen down when you're finished.
(Observe students and give feedback.)

10. (Write on the board:)

> 1. **No, only girls played at the picnic.**
> 2. **No, girls played only at the picnic.**
> 3. **No, girls only played at the picnic.**

- Check your work. Here's what you should have for each item. Raise your hand if you got everything right.

11. Remember how the word **only** works. Its position in the sentence makes a big difference in what the sentence means.

### EXERCISE 2   Critiquing
**Disagreement/Agreement**

1. Find part B.
- (Teacher reference:)

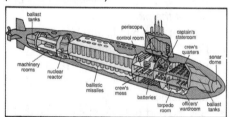

- There's a diagram of a nuclear-powered submarine, some definitions, and some statements. The definitions are true. Some of the statements are inaccurate.
- Look at the diagram of the submarine and read the definitions. They tell meanings of some labels on the diagram. The front of the submarine is called **forward.** The sonar dome is at the front of the submarine.

2. Statement 1: **The place where the crew sleeps is in front of the place where the periscope is located.**
- Raise your hand when you know whether that statement is accurate or inaccurate.
- Everybody, is statement 1 accurate or inaccurate? (Signal.) *Accurate.*
- What's the name of the place where the crew sleeps? (Signal.) *Crew's quarters.*

3. Write your paragraph for statement 1. When you give facts in your paragraph, tell where the places are. Maybe you can tell what is between the places or what is just in front of one of the places.
- First, tell about the crew's quarters. Use the names that are shown in the diagram. Write parallel sentences. Put your pen down when you're finished.
(Observe students and give feedback.)
- Here's a good paragraph for statement 1:
  > Statement 1 indicates **that** the place where the crew sleeps is in front of the place where the periscope is located. That statement is accurate. The crew's quarters are in front of the captain's stateroom. The periscope room is behind the captain's stateroom.
- (Call on several students to read their paragraph. Praise good accounts.)

4. Your turn: Write your paragraph for statement 2. Put your pen down when you're finished.
(Observe students and give feedback.)
- Here is a good paragraph:
  > Statement 2 indicates **that** the place where the crew eats is not on the same level as the captain's stateroom. That statement is accurate. The crew's mess is below the captain's stateroom.
- (Call on several students to read their paragraph. Praise good accounts.)

### EXERCISE 3   Unclear Words
**Pronouns**

1. Find part C.
- Each underlined sentence has an unclear word. You're going to rewrite that sentence by replacing the unclear word with words that are specific and clear.

2. Rewrite the underlined sentences in part C. Put your pen down when you've finished.
(Observe students and give feedback.)

3. Here's the sentence you should have written for item 1:
  > As the sun rose over the desert, **the desert** turned pink.
- Here's the sentence you should have written for item 2:
  > **The violin** produced lovely music.

- Here's the sentence you should have written for item 3:
|| **The pond** was full of cows.
- Raise your hand if you got everything right.

### EXERCISE 4    Fact/Opinion

1. Find part D. ✔
- Follow along as I read what's in the box:

> - *Facts* are statements that can be proved. Facts can be proved with *statistics, numbers,* or *examples.*
> - *Opinions* are personal beliefs or feelings. Opinions *can't* be proved.

2. What do we call statements that can be proved with statistics or examples? (Signal.) *Facts.*
- What are personal beliefs or feelings that can't be proved? (Signal.) *Opinions.*
3. Listen: **The Great Wall of China is more than 1,400 miles long.** Is that statement a fact or opinion? (Signal.) *Fact.*
- Yes, you can prove the statement by measuring the Great Wall of China, so it's a fact.
- Listen: **The Great Wall of China is the greatest human achievement of all time.** Is that statement a fact or opinion? (Signal.) *Opinion.*
- It's an opinion because you can't prove the statement. It's just a feeling or belief.
4. I'll read the instructions: **For each statement, write *fact* or *opinion*. Write *fact* if the statement can be proved. Write *opinion* if it's just a feeling or belief that can't be proved.**
- Statement 1: **Last year, teenagers bought more than 20 million CDs.**
- Is that a fact or an opinion? (Signal.) *Fact.*
- Why is it a fact? (Call on a student. Idea: *It can be proved by checking the number.*)
5. Statement 2: **Most of the CDs teenagers buy are just loud noise.**
- Is that a fact or an opinion? (Signal.) *Opinion.*

- Why is it an opinion? (Call on a student. Ideas: *It can't be proved; it's just a feeling or belief.*)
6. Do the items. Put your pen down when you're finished.
(Observe students and give feedback.)
7. Check your work.
- Statement 1: **Last year, teenagers bought more than 20 million CDs.** Fact or opinion? (Signal.) *Fact.*
- Statement 2: **Most of the CDs teenagers buy are just loud noise.** Fact or opinion? (Signal.) *Opinion.*
- Statement 3: **The average CD costs about 15 dollars.** Fact or opinion? (Signal.) *Fact.*
- Statement 4: **Some CDs cost as much as 30 dollars.** Fact or opinion? (Signal.) *Fact.*
- Statement 5: **No CD is worth 30 dollars!** Fact or opinion? (Signal.) *Opinion.*
- Statement 6: **CDs weren't available 100 years ago.** Fact or opinion? (Signal.) *Fact.*
8. Correct any mistakes.
(Observe students and give feedback.)

### EXERCISE 5    Independent Work

1. Do the independent work for lesson 18.
2. (Before beginning the next lesson, check students' independent work. Spot-check the rest of the lesson.)
*Key for independent work:*
*Part E*
|| *was not, she would, did not*
|| *{cannot/can not}, had not*

# Grade 5 Language Arts Textbook

**Lesson 18**

**A**

Correct the first statement in each item by writing a sentence that uses the words **no** and **only**.

1. Girls and boys _played_ at the picnic.
   Girls played at the picnic.
2. Girls _played_ at the picnic and in the cabin.
   Girls played at the picnic.
3. Girls _played and talked_ at the picnic.
   Girls played at the picnic.

**B** *Source: Diagram of a Submarine*

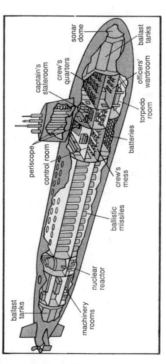

**Definitions:** captain's stateroom—place where the captain sleeps

officers' wardroom—place where the officers eat and sleep

crew's quarters—place where the crew sleeps

crew's mess—place where the crew eats

*Statements*

1. The place where the crew sleeps is in front of the place where the periscope is located.
2. The place where the crew eats is not on the same level as the captain's stateroom.

*Outline diagrams*

Statement ___ indicates that ___. ✗ That statement is inaccurate. [Give fact.]

Statement ___ indicates that ___. = That statement is accurate. [Give fact.]

*Lesson 18* — 48

---

**C**

Rewrite the underlined sentences so that the unclear word is clear.

1. As the sun rose over the desert, it turned pink. The desert is so beautiful when it is that color.
2. Jerry played violin in the orchestra. It produced lovely music.
   He didn't want to play any other violin.
3. We got to the pond by going through a wheat field. It was full of cows.
   Some of them were swimming.

**D**

- **Facts** are statements that can be proved. Facts can be proved with *statistics, numbers,* or *examples.*
- **Opinions** are personal beliefs or feelings. Opinions *can't* be proved.

For each statement, write **fact** or **opinion**. Write **opinion** if it's just a feeling or belief that can't be proved. Write **fact** if the statement can be proved.

1. Last year, teenagers bought more than 20 million CDs.
2. Most of the CDs teenagers buy are just loud noise.
3. The average CD costs about 15 dollars.
4. Some CDs cost as much as 30 dollars.
5. No CD is worth 30 dollars!
6. CDs weren't available 100 years ago.

**Independent Work**

**E** The passage has five contractions. Write the two words that make up each contraction.

She wasn't tired, but she had run a long distance. She told the others that she'd win the race, but nobody believed her. She was only 11 years old. All the other runners were in their teens. She didn't look like a runner, but you can't always tell how well somebody runs by looking at them. She went through the four mile course so fast that some of the runners hadn't completed half of it by the time she finished. Five years after this race she did the same thing in the Olympics. She won gold.

*Lesson 18* — 49

# Literature Strand Overview

The *Reading Mastery* Literature strand includes six full-year programs (Grades K–5) that provide supplementary literature for the Reading strand. The Literature strand for each grade consists of a Literature Guide for you and either a Literature Collection (Grades K–1) or a Literature Anthology (Grades 2–5) for the students.

| Teacher Materials | K | 1 | 2 | 3 | 4 | 5 |
|---|---|---|---|---|---|---|
| Literature Guide | ◆ | ◆ | ◆ | ◆ | ◆ | ◆ |
| **Student Materials** | | | | | | |
| Literature Collection | ◆ | ◆ | | | | |
| Literature Anthology | | | ◆ | ◆ | ◆ | ◆ |

The Literature strand provides additional stories, poems, and plays for students to read and enjoy after they finish a certain number of lessons in the Reading strand. In Grades K and 1, for example, selections from the Literature Collection are presented after every fifth lesson in the Reading strand. In Grades 2–5, selections from the Literature Anthology are presented after every tenth lesson in the Reading strand.

The Literature Collections for Grades K and 1 consist of individual softbound books with relatively simple text and colorful illustrations. The Literature Anthologies for Grades 2–5 are hardbound books with fewer illustrations and more text. A complete list of Literature selections for each grade appears in the next part of this Series Guide.

## Literature Activities for Grades K and 1

The Literature Collections for Grades K and 1 feature stories that are fun to read aloud and that invite participation. The stories often have predictable or rhyming text and interesting illustrations. In Grade K, you read all the stories aloud. In Grade 1, you read some stories, and the students read others.

The Literature Guides for Grades K and 1 include additional activities for each story. In Grade K, for example, you present specified comprehension questions while reading the story. In Grade 1, students read lists of story words, answer comprehension questions, and read the stories individually. They also take the stories home to read to their families.

## Literature Activities for Grades 2–5

The selections in the Literature Anthologies for Grades 2–5 include classic and modern fiction, poems, and plays. Many of the selections are by well-known children's writers.

Each Literature Anthology story is accompanied by pre-reading and post-reading activities, such as vocabulary definitions, story background, comprehension items, and writing assignments. Directions for presenting these activities appear in the Literature Guide. Students can read the stories either aloud or silently.

In Grades 2 and 3, the student activities appear on blackline masters in the Literature Guide. In Grades 4 and 5, the activities appear in the Literature Anthology. Typical activities include the following:

- **New Vocabulary Words and Definitions**
  These activities are similar to the word-practice and vocabulary routines in the Reading strand. Students read lists of vocabulary words that will appear in the stories and learn what they mean. Then students practice using the words in sentences.

- **Story Background**
  These passages provide historical or literary information that enhances students' understanding of the Literature Anthology stories. As students read the passage aloud, you present comprehension questions from the Literature Guide.

■ **Focus Questions**

These questions help students focus on the important concepts and themes of each story. Students read the focus questions aloud and think about them as they read the story.

■ **Story Reading**

Depending on grade level and ability, students can read the Literature Anthology stories either aloud or silently. Students can also read the stories in pairs or in small groups.

■ **Story Questions**

These questions are often closely aligned to the focus questions. Students answer the questions either orally or in writing after finishing the story.

■ **Retelling the Story**

Students retell the story as a group. One student retells the first part of the story, then another student tells the next part, and so forth.

■ **Literary Elements**

Students learn about basic literary elements—such as character, setting, and plot—and identify those elements in the stories.

■ **Discussion Topics**

These activities present story-related topics for students to discuss as a class or in small groups. Topics include story themes, conflicts, and dilemmas.

■ **Writing Ideas**

These assignments span a variety of writing skills, from composing letters to assuming the perspective of a story character. Students can complete the assignments individually or as a group.

# Literature Selections and Sample Lessons

This section provides a complete list of selections for each grade of the Literature strand. Sample lessons are provided for Grades K, 2, and 4. Use the table below to locate the material for each grade.

| Grades | Page |
|--------|------|
| K | 119 |
| 1 | 131 |
| 2 | 132 |
| 3 | 149 |
| 4 | 150 |
| 5 | 166 |

## Grade K Literature

Grade K Literature contains 10 stories, each of which is presented at three different points in the Reading strand. For example, the story for Literature lesson 1 is presented at lessons 20, 25, and 30 in the Reading strand. All stories at the Grade K level are read aloud to the children; they are not expected to read the stories themselves. The stories and authors for Grade K Literature are listed below.

| Lesson | Title | Author |
|--------|-------|--------|
| 1 | What Are You Called? | Honey Andersen and Bill Reinholtd |
| 2 | Dog Went for a Walk | Sally Farrell Odgers |
| 3 | Goodnight | Penelope Coad |
| 4 | Farmer Schnuck | Brenda Parkes |
| 5 | This and That | Vic Warren |
| 6 | Henrietta's First Winter | Rob Lewis |
| 7 | Maxie's Cat | Carol Carrick |
| 8 | The Perfects | Marjorie Weinman Sharmat |
| 9 | Nibbly Mouse | David Drew |
| 10 | Little Dinosaur | Trevor Wilson |

The following sample story from Grade K, *This and That*, is presented after lessons 80, 85, and 90 in the Reading strand. The story introduces different compound words. The questions that you ask change after the first presentation of the story.

Take some **butter**.
Add a **fly**.
Now you have a...

butterfly.

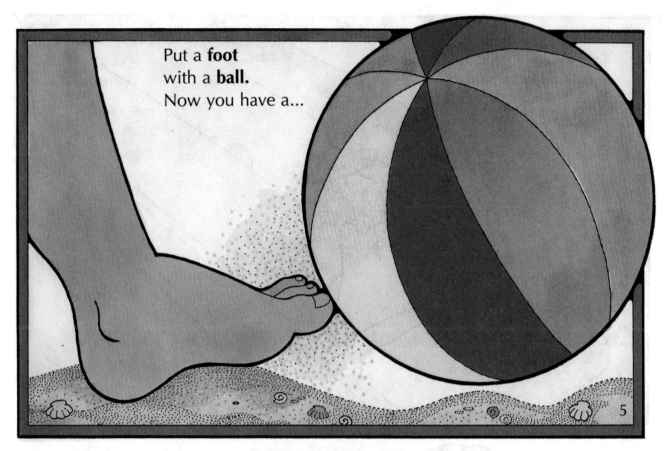

Put a **foot**
with a **ball.**
Now you have a...

football.

Take a **pan**
and a **cake**.
Now you have a...

7

8

**pancake.**

When there is **rain**,
add a **bow.**
Now you have a...

rainbow.

Add a **cup**
and a **board.**
Now you have a...

11

cupboard.

12

Put a **star**
with a **fish.**
Now you have a...

13

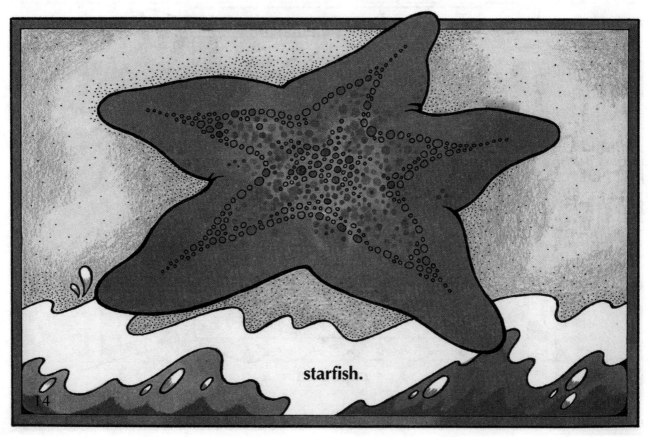

**starfish.**

14

Take a **book.**
Find the **end.**
Now you have a...

THE END.

DOGS

15

bookend.

16

## LITERATURE LESSON 5
# This and That

Written by Vic Warren
Illustrated by Olivia Cole

*This and That* introduces different compound words and shows pictures of the component words (Take some **butter.** Add a **fly.** Now you have a . . . **butterfly.**) Like the other books in the first set, *This and That* promotes participation of children when they put the component words together and take the compound words apart (What words did you put together to get **butterfly?**). Also like the others in the first set, *This and That* works on skills that are important for the beginning reader.

|  | Follows *Reading Mastery* Lesson |
|---|---|
| **First Reading** | 80 |
| **Second Reading** | 85 |
| **Third Reading** | 90 |

## First Reading Only

I'll read the whole story and show you the pictures. Then I'll ask you questions.

| Page 2 | • (Show picture.) I bet you know all about adding numbers. But what do you know about adding words? |
|---|---|
| Page 3 | • (Show picture.) Take some **butter.** Add a **fly.** Now you have a . . . |
| Page 4 | • (Show picture.) **butterfly.** |
| Page 5 | • (Show picture.) Put a **foot** with a **ball.** Now you have a . . . |
| Page 6 | • (Show picture.) **football.** |

| | |
|---|---|
| Page 7 | • (Show picture.)<br>Take a **pan**<br>and a **cake.**<br>Now you have a . . . |
| Page 8 | • (Show picture.)<br>**pancake.** |
| Page 9 | • (Show picture.)<br>When there is **rain,**<br>add a **bow.**<br>Now you have a . . . |
| Page 10 | • (Show picture.)<br>**rainbow.** |
| Page 11 | • (Show picture.)<br>Add a **cup**<br>and a **board.**<br>Now you have a . . . |
| Page 12 | • (Show picture.)<br>**cupboard.** |
| Page 13 | • (Show picture.)<br>Put a **star**<br>with a **fish.**<br>Now you have a . . . |
| Page 14 | • (Show picture.)<br>**starfish.** |
| Page 15 | • (Show picture.)<br>Take a **book.**<br>Find the **end.**<br>Now you have a . . . |
| Page 16 | • (Show picture.)<br>**bookend.** |

## All Readings

Now we'll read that book again.

| | |
|---|---|
| Page 3 | • (Show picture.)<br>Take some **butter.** Add a **fly.** Now you have a . . . *Butterfly.*<br>• What's on that butter? *A fly.*<br>What funny word could you get by adding **butter** and **fly?**<br>*Butterfly.* |
| Page 4 | • (Show picture.) What is that? *Butterfly.* |

# Grade K Literature Guide

| | |
|---|---|
| Page 5 | • (Show picture.)<br>    Put a **foot** with a **ball**. Now you have a . . . *Football.*<br>• What is that foot touching? *A ball.*<br>  What funny word could you get by adding **foot** and **ball?** *Football.* |
| Page 6 | • (Show picture.) What is that? *Football.* |
| Page 7 | • (Show picture.)<br>    Take a **pan** and a **cake**. Now you have a . . . *Pancake.*<br>• What is the pan touching? *A cake.*<br>  What funny word could you get by adding **pan** and **cake?** *Pancake.* |
| Page 8 | • (Show picture.) What is that? *Pancake.* |
| Page 9 | • (Show picture.)<br>    When there is **rain,** add a **bow**. Now you have a . . . *Rainbow.*<br>• What is that in her hair? *A bow.*<br>  Is the rain touching that bow? *Yes.*<br>  What funny word could you get by adding **rain** and **bow?** *Rainbow.* |
| Page 10 | • (Show picture.) What is that? *Rainbow.* |
| Page 11 | • (Show picture.)<br>    Add a **cup** and a **board.** Now you have a . . . *Cupboard.*<br>• What is the cup touching? *A board.*<br>  What funny word could you get by adding **cup** and **board?** *Cupboard.* |
| Page 12 | • (Show picture.) What is that? *Cupboard.* |
| Page 13 | • (Show picture.)<br>    Put a **star** with a **fish**. Now you have a . . . *Starfish.*<br>• What is in front of that fish? *A star.*<br>  What funny word could you get by adding a **star** and a **fish?** *Starfish.* |
| Page 14 | • (Show picture.) What is that? *Starfish.* |
| Page 15 | • (Show picture.)<br>    Take a **book.** Find the **end.** Now you have a . . . *Bookend.*<br>• The words in the book say "The end."<br>  What do they say? *The end.*<br>  What funny word could you get by adding **book** and **end?** *Bookend.* |
| Page 16 | • (Show picture.) What is that? *Bookend.* |

## Third Reading

(Ask Children to take the compound words apart.) What words did you put together to make butterfly?

22    Grade K Literature Lesson 5

# Grade 1 Literature

Grade 1 Literature contains nine stories, each of which is presented at three different points in the Reading strand. For example, the story for Literature Lesson 1 is presented at lessons 5, 55, and 105 in the Reading strand. In the first presentation, you read the story and ask questions as students follow along in their own books. In the second presentation, students first read a list of words from the story and then read the story as a group. In the third presentation, students read the story individually and answer comprehension questions when they're done. Then they take the story home to read to family members.

| Lesson | Title | Author |
|--------|-------|--------|
| 1 | *One Little Kitten* | Tana Hoban |
| 2 | *The Carrot Seed* | Ruth Krauss |
| 3 | *Who Took the Farmer's Hat?* | Joan L. Nŏdset |
| 4 | *A Kiss for Little Bear* | Else Holmelund Minarik |
| 5 | *Molly's Bracelet* | Isabel Bissett |
| 6 | *There Stood Our Dog* | Anne Houghton |
| 7 | *Fat Cat Tompkin* | Diana Noonan |
| 8 | *In the Forest* | Stephen Ray and Kathleen Murdoch |
| 9 | *The Perfects* | Marjorie Weinman Sharmat |

## Grade 2 Literature

Grade 2 Literature contains 16 lessons, which are generally presented after every tenth lesson in the Reading strand. The first Literature lesson introduces literary elements, such as character, setting, and plot. For the remaining Literature lessons, students read one or two selections in the Literature Anthology and complete blackline masters from the Literature Guide. Lesson 9 includes a read-to story that appears in the Literature Guide.

| Lesson | Title | Author | Genre |
|---|---|---|---|
| 1 | *Introduction of Literary Elements* | | |
| 2 | *Stephanie's Ponytail* | Robert Munsch | Humorous fiction |
| 3 | *George at the Zoo* | Sally George | Animal story |
| 4-1 | *A House with a Star Inside* | Retold by Melissa Heckler | Riddle story |
| 4-2 | *Remember* | Pamela Mordecai | Poem |
| 5 | *Pop's Truck* | Honey Anderson and Bill Reinholtd | Realistic fiction |
| 6 | *Trixie* | Rick Brownell | Animal story |
| 7 | *The Three Wishes* | Margot Zemach | Folktale |
| 8 | *Tom's Friend* | Pat Reynolds | Animal story |
| 9-1 | *The Case of Natty Nat* | Donald Sobol | Read-to |
| 9-2 | *Swap* | Carol Diggory Shields | Poem |
| 10-1 | *The Thirsty Crows* | Faye W. Daggett | Fable |
| 10-2 | *Rabbit Poem* | Pamela Mordecai | Poem |
| 11 | *Moonwalker* | Carol Diggory Shields | Poem |
| 12 | *See the Rabbits—Part 1* | Harvey Cleaver | Realistic fiction |
| 13 | *See the Rabbits—Part 2* | Harvey Cleaver | Realistic fiction |
| 14 | *The Proud Crow* | Adapted by Fran Lehr | Play |
| 15 | *The Fox and the Crow* | Retold by Faye W. Daggett | Fable |
| 16 | *The Magic Teakettle* | Harriet Winfield | Folktale |

The following sample play from Grade 2, *The Proud Crow,* is presented after Lesson 120 in the Reading strand.

Students begin the lesson by studying a list of vocabulary words that appear in the play. After you explain important features of plays, the students read the play aloud. Then students present the play, using costumes, settings, and props.

# the **Proud** crow

Adapted by Fran Lehr from a fable by Aesop
Illustrated by Joel Snyder

CHARACTERS

NARRATOR
MISS CROW
MR. FOX
3 STALL KEEPERS
TOWNSPEOPLE

SCENE 1

Time:
Once upon a time.

Setting:
A marketplace, with three stalls, one
displaying a pile of vegetables, one
displaying strings of sausage, and one
displaying balls and slices of cheese. TOWNSPEOPLE,
most with baskets on their arms, bustle from stall to stall.
At each stall, a STALL KEEPER stands. All are shouting
loudly–and at the same time:

STALL KEEPER 1:
(Holding high several vegetables)

Fresh vegetables! Get your fresh vegetables here! Freshest
in town! Only a few pennies a pound!

STALL KEEPER 2:
(Holding a long string of sausages)

Sausages! Juicy sausages! Get your sausages here!

STALL KEEPER 3:
(Holding up large pieces of cheese in each hand)

Yummy cheeses! I've got big cheese and little cheeses!
Blue cheese and yellow cheese and orange cheese and red
cheese!

The TOWNSPEOPLE start to buy from the STALL KEEPERS, and the shouting stops. From
stage right, NARRATOR enters and stands near the front of the stage.

**153**

NARRATOR:

Once upon a time, in a small village in a far away place, there lived a large, silly crow.

(MISS CROW enters at the back of the stage.)

Miss crow was very proud. She was proud of her shiny black feathers.

(MISS CROW smiles and pats her feathers.)

She was proud of her dainty beak.

(MISS CROW rubs her beak.)

She was proud of her bright, shining eyes.

(MISS CROW flutters her eyes.)

But most of all, Miss Crow was proud of her singing voice.

(MISS CROW lifts her head, closes her eyes, and opens her beak very, very wide.)

MISS CROW:

CAW–W–W–W–W!

(Townspeople AND Stall Keepers all cover their ears with their hands and moan MISS CROW is so pleased with her singing that she does not see them. She smiles and bows.

MISS CROW:

Thank you, thank you! Shall I sing more?

TOWNSPEOPLE and STALL KEEPERS:

NO!!!

154

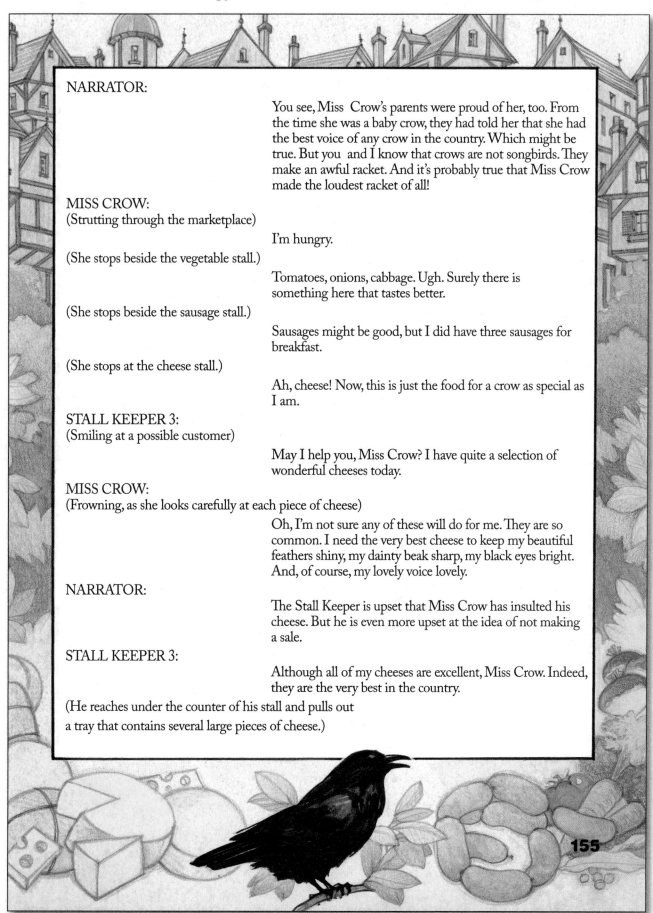

**NARRATOR:**

You see, Miss Crow's parents were proud of her, too. From the time she was a baby crow, they had told her that she had the best voice of any crow in the country. Which might be true. But you and I know that crows are not songbirds. They make an awful racket. And it's probably true that Miss Crow made the loudest racket of all!

**MISS CROW:**
(Strutting through the marketplace)

I'm hungry.

(She stops beside the vegetable stall.)

Tomatoes, onions, cabbage. Ugh. Surely there is something here that tastes better.

(She stops beside the sausage stall.)

Sausages might be good, but I did have three sausages for breakfast.

(She stops at the cheese stall.)

Ah, cheese! Now, this is just the food for a crow as special as I am.

**STALL KEEPER 3:**
(Smiling at a possible customer)

May I help you, Miss Crow? I have quite a selection of wonderful cheeses today.

**MISS CROW:**
(Frowning, as she looks carefully at each piece of cheese)

Oh, I'm not sure any of these will do for me. They are so common. I need the very best cheese to keep my beautiful feathers shiny, my dainty beak sharp, my black eyes bright. And, of course, my lovely voice lovely.

**NARRATOR:**

The Stall Keeper is upset that Miss Crow has insulted his cheese. But he is even more upset at the idea of not making a sale.

**STALL KEEPER 3:**

Although all of my cheeses are excellent, Miss Crow. Indeed, they are the very best in the country.

(He reaches under the counter of his stall and pulls out a tray that contains several large pieces of cheese.)

155

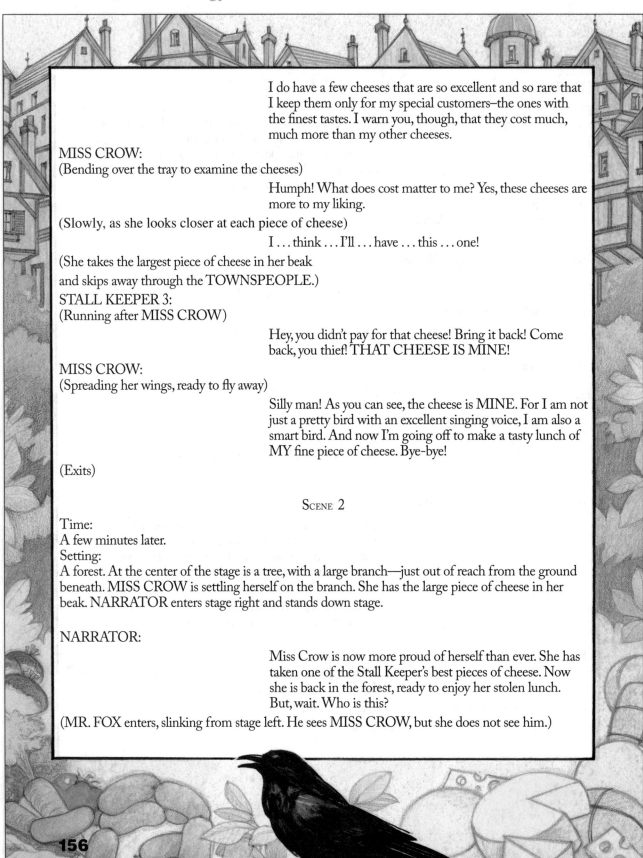

I do have a few cheeses that are so excellent and so rare that I keep them only for my special customers–the ones with the finest tastes. I warn you, though, that they cost much, much more than my other cheeses.

MISS CROW:
(Bending over the tray to examine the cheeses)

Humph! What does cost matter to me? Yes, these cheeses are more to my liking.

(Slowly, as she looks closer at each piece of cheese)

I ... think ... I'll ... have ... this ... one!

(She takes the largest piece of cheese in her beak and skips away through the TOWNSPEOPLE.)

STALL KEEPER 3:
(Running after MISS CROW)

Hey, you didn't pay for that cheese! Bring it back! Come back, you thief! THAT CHEESE IS MINE!

MISS CROW:
(Spreading her wings, ready to fly away)

Silly man! As you can see, the cheese is MINE. For I am not just a pretty bird with an excellent singing voice, I am also a smart bird. And now I'm going off to make a tasty lunch of MY fine piece of cheese. Bye-bye!

(Exits)


Scene 2

Time:
A few minutes later.
Setting:
A forest. At the center of the stage is a tree, with a large branch—just out of reach from the ground beneath. MISS CROW is settling herself on the branch. She has the large piece of cheese in her beak. NARRATOR enters stage right and stands down stage.

NARRATOR:

Miss Crow is now more proud of herself than ever. She has taken one of the Stall Keeper's best pieces of cheese. Now she is back in the forest, ready to enjoy her stolen lunch. But, wait. Who is this?

(MR. FOX enters, slinking from stage left. He sees MISS CROW, but she does not see him.)

156

MR. FOX:
(In a loud whisper)

It's past my lunchtime, and I'm very hungry.

(He looks up at MISS CROW and smiles slyly.)

And there's Miss Crow with a piece of excellent cheese. Too excellent for a silly crow, but perfect for a clever fox such as I. Now, how can I get it away from her?

(He frowns a bit, thinking.)

I can't climb the tree and grab it,

(He frowns deeper.)

because I can't climb trees.

(Thinking harder)

I can't throw a rock and knock it from her beak,

(Looking around and frowning)

because there are no rocks and I can't throw.

(His face brightens.)

I'll have to make her drop it. And I know just the trick to do it!

(He slinks beneath the tree and calls sweetly)

Good day to you, Miss Crow. I hope you won't mind if I stop to tell you how splendid you look today?

MISS CROW:
(Fluffing out her feathers and sitting taller on the branch)

Not at all, Mr. Fox. I think I'm looking rather grand myself.

MR. FOX:

Oh, more than grand—if you don't mind me saying so—more than grand. Your feathers are especially shiny today! Your beak is especially dainty. Your eyes are especially bright—like jewels!

MISS CROW:
(Sitting even taller)

Yes, yes. That's all true.

**157**

MR. FOX:

> And from what everyone says, your voice is more beautiful than your feathers; daintier than your beak; lovelier than your eyes. I don't suppose you would be willing to let me hear you sing? Perhaps one little song?

(Turning to the audience and winking)
MISS CROW:
(So taken in by the flattery that she can barely sit still on the branch)

> Well, it is my lunchtime. But I suppose I can manage one little song.

(She throws back her head and opens her beak wide.)

> CAW–W–W–W–W!

(The piece of cheese falls to the ground, right in front of MR. FOX.)
MR. FOX:
(Grabbing the cheese)

> Thank you, Miss Crow! For giving me this excellent cheese, I will give you an excellent piece of advice: Never believe flattery!

158

(He skips off, eating the cheese.)
NARRATOR:

So Miss Crow learned a very important lesson: Too much pride can make you look like a fool.

(Exits)
MISS CROW:
(Sits on the tree branch, looking sad–and hungry.)

## Literature Lesson 14

To be presented with Lesson 120
Anthology page 153

# *The Proud Crow*

Adapted by Fran Lehr from a fable by Aesop
Illustrated by Joel Snyder

Theme: Vanity

*The Proud Crow* is a play about a crow that learns an important lesson.

## Materials

> 1 copy of the literature anthology for each student
> 1 copy of blackline master 14A for each student
> Modest costumes, stage settings (3 stalls for scene 1, forest for scene 2), and props (for example, food items for market stalls, baskets for shoppers, pieces of cheese.)

## Presenting the Play

1. (Make a copy of blackline master 14A for each student. Distribute copies to students.)
2. We're going to read a play several times and then put it on. When we put on the play, students will act the parts of characters in the play. Those students will read the lines for the characters they play.
3. Look at your worksheet.
- These are some of the words in the play that you may not know. The meanings are written for the words. (Call on individual students to read the words and their meanings.)

> (Answer Key:)
> 1. **narrator** The narrator of a play is one who tells the story to the audience.
> 2. **bustle** Things that bustle are busy moving about.
> 3. **marketplace** A place where people buy all sorts of things.
> 4. **insult** When you insult someone, you say something about that person that is not very nice.
> 5. **excellent** Things that are excellent are very, very good.
> 6. **rare** Rare things are hard to find and not common.
> 7. **customers** People who buy things at a store are customers.
> 8. **splendid Splendid** is another word for **excellent.**
> 9. **dainty** Dainty things are very fine.
> 10. **flattery** When you flatter people, you tell them how great they are, even though you may not be telling the truth.

**4.** Find page 153 in your anthology. ✔

• A play is written a different way from a story. A play has headings. The headings tell who is talking or doing something. The passage that follows the heading tells what the person says or does. The first part of the play tells who the characters are, when and where the play takes place and what is happening when the first scene opens. The characters for this play are the narrator, Miss Crow, Mr. Fox, 3 stall keepers, and townspeople.

• The narrator is a character who talks to the audience but is not actually a character in the play. The narrator tells things that help you understand what's going on in the play. Follow along while I read the first part of the play.

• Scene 1
Time: Once upon a time. When does the play take place? (Call on a student. Idea: *Once upon a time.*)

• Setting. A marketplace, with three stalls, one displaying a pile of vegetables, one displaying strings of sausage, and one displaying balls and slices of cheese. TOWNSPEOPLE, most with baskets on their arms, bustle from stall to stall. At each stall, a STALL KEEPER stands. All are shouting loudly—and at the same time.

• Where does the play take place? (Call on a student. Idea: *At a marketplace.*)

• How many stalls are in the play? *3.*

• (Direct students to read Scene 1 of the play aloud.)

- (Teacher reference:)

---

**Scene 1**

Time:
*Once upon a time.*

Setting:
*A marketplace, with three stalls, one displaying
a pile of vegetables, one displaying strings of
sausage, and one displaying balls and slices of
cheese.* TOWNSPEOPLE, *most with baskets on
their arms, bustle from stall to stall. At each stall,
a* STALL KEEPER *stands. All are shouting loudly—
and at the same time:*

**STALL KEEPER 1:**
*(Holding high several vegetables)*

Fresh vegetables! Get your fresh vegetables
here! Freshest in town! Only a few pennies
a pound!

**STALL KEEPER 2:**
*(Holding a long string of sausages)*

Sausages! Juicy sausages! Get your sausages
here!

**STALL KEEPER 3:**
*(Holding up large pieces of cheese in
each hand)*

Yummy cheeses! I've got big cheeses and
little cheeses! Blue cheese and yellow cheese
and orange cheese and red cheese!

*The* TOWNSPEOPLE *start to buy from the* STALL
KEEPERS, *and the shouting stops. From stage
right,* NARRATOR *enters and stands near the front
of the stage.*

---

**NARRATOR:**

Once upon a time, in a small village in a far away place, there lived a large, silly crow.

(Miss Crow *enters at the back of the stage.*)

Miss Crow was very proud. She was proud of her shiny black feathers.

(Miss Crow *smiles and pats her feathers.*)

She was proud of her dainty beak.

(Miss Crow *rubs her beak.*)

She was proud of her bright, shining eyes.

(Miss Crow *flutters her eyes.*)

But most of all, Miss Crow was proud of her singing voice.

(Miss Crow *lifts her head, closes her eyes, and opens her beak very, very wide.*)

**MISS CROW:**

CAW-W-W-W-W!

(TOWNSPEOPLE, STALL KEEPERS, *and* NARRATOR *all cover their ears with their hands and moan.* MISS CROW *is so pleased with her singing that she does not see them. She smiles and bows.*)

**MISS CROW:**

Thank you, thank you! Shall I sing more?

**TOWNSPEOPLE AND STALL KEEPERS:**

NO!!!

**NARRATOR:**

You see, Miss Crow's parents were proud of her, too. From the time she was a baby crow, they had told her that she had the best voice of any crow in the country. Which might be true. But you and I know that crows are not songbirds. They make an awful racket. And it's probably true that Miss Crow made the loudest racket of all!

**MISS CROW:**
(*Strutting through the market place*)

I'm hungry.

(*She stops beside the vegetable stall.*)

Tomatoes, onions, cabbage. Ugh. Surely there is something here that tastes better.

(*She stops beside the sausage stall.*)

Sausages might be good, but I did have three sausages for breakfast.

(*She stops beside the cheese stall.*)

Ah, cheese! Now, this is just the food for a crow as special as I am.

**STALL KEEPER 3:**
(*Smiling at a possible customer*)

May I help you, Miss Crow? I have quite a selection of wonderful cheese today.

**MISS CROW:**
(*Frowning, as she looks carefully at each piece of cheese*)

Oh, I'm not sure any of these will do for me. They are so common. I need the very best cheese to keep my beautiful feathers shiny, my dainty beak sharp, my black eyes bright. And, of course, my lovely voice lovely.

**NARRATOR:**

The Stall Keeper is upset that Miss Crow has insulted his cheeses. But he is even more upset at the idea of not making a sale.

**STALL KEEPER 3:**

Although *all* of my cheeses are excellent, Miss Crow. Indeed, they are the very best in the country.

(*He reaches under the counter of his stall and pulls out a tray that contains several large pieces of cheese.*)

I do have a few cheeses that are so excellent and so rare that I keep them only for my special customers—the ones with the finest tastes. I warn you, though, that they cost much, much more than my other cheeses.

**MISS CROW:**
(*Bending over the tray to examine the cheeses*)

Humph! What does cost matter to me? Yes, these cheeses are more to my liking.

(*Slowly, as she looks closer at each piece of cheese*)

I . . . think . . . I'll have . . . this . . . one!

(*She takes the largest piece of cheese in her beak and skips away through the* TOWNSPEOPLE.)

**STALL KEEPER 3:**
(*Running after* MISS CROW)

Hey, you didn't pay for that cheese! Bring it back! Come back, you thief! THAT CHEESE IS MINE!

**MISS CROW:**
(*Spreading her wings, ready to fly away*)

Silly man! As you can see, the cheese is MINE. For I am not just a pretty bird with an excellent singing voice, I am also a smart bird. And now I'm going off to make a tasty lunch of MY fine piece of cheese. Bye-bye!

(*Exits*)

**5.** That's the end of scene 1. Where did that scene take place? Idea: *At a marketplace.*

- The next scene is scene 2. It does not take place in the marketplace. Follow along while I read the first part of scene 2.
- Time: A few minutes later.
  How soon does this scene take place after the other scene ends? *A few minutes later.*
- Setting: A forest. At the center of the stage is a tree, with a large branch—just out of reach from the ground beneath. MISS CROW is settling herself on the branch. She has the large piece of cheese in her beak. NARRATOR enters stage right and stands down stage.
  Where is the setting for this scene? *A forest.*
- Who is in the scene besides the narrator? *Mr. Fox, Miss Crow.*
- (Direct students to read scene 2 of the play aloud.)
- (Teacher reference:)

---

**SCENE 2**

Time:
*A few minutes later.*

Setting:
*A forest. At the center of the stage is a tree, with a large branch—just out of reach from the ground beneath.* MISS CROW *is settling herself on the branch. She has the large piece of cheese in her beak.* NARRATOR *enters stage right and stands down stage.*

**NARRATOR:**

Miss Crow is now more proud of herself than ever. She has taken one of the Stall Keeper's best pieces of cheese. Now she is back in the forest, ready to enjoy her stolen lunch. But, wait. Who is this?

(MR. FOX *enters, slinking from stage left. He sees* MISS CROW, *but she does not see him.*)

**MR. FOX:**
(*In a loud whisper*)

It's past my lunchtime, and I'm very hungry.

(*He looks up at* MISS CROW *and smiles slyly.*)

And there's Miss Crow with a piece of excellent cheese. Too excellent for a silly crow, but perfect for a clever fox such as I. Now, how can I get it away from her?

(*He frowns a bit, thinking.*)

I can't climb the tree and grab it,

(*He frowns deeper.*)

because I can't climb trees.

---

**Grade 2** Literature Lesson 14          **109**

(*Thinking harder*)

I can't throw a rock and knock it from her beak,

(*Looking around and frowning*)

because there are no rocks and I can't throw.

(*His face brightens.*)

I'll have to make her drop it. And I know just the trick to do it!

(*He slinks beneath the tree and calls sweetly*)

Good day to you, Miss Crow. I hope you won't mind if I stop to tell you how splendid you look today?

**MISS CROW:**

(*Fluffing out her feathers and sitting taller on the branch*)

Not at all, Mr. Fox. I think I'm looking rather grand myself.

**MR. FOX:**

Oh, more than grand—if you don't mind me saying so—more than grand. Your feathers are especially shiny today! Your beak is especially dainty. Your eyes are especially bright—like jewels!

**MISS CROW:**
(*Sitting even taller*)

Yes, yes. That's all true.

**MR. FOX:**

And from what everyone says, your voice is more beautiful than your feathers; daintier than your beak; lovelier than your eyes. I don't suppose you would be willing to let me hear you sing? Perhaps one little song?

(*Turning to the audience and winking*)

**MISS CROW:**
(*So taken in by the flattery that she can barely sit still on the branch*)

Well, it is my lunchtime. But I suppose I can manage one little song.

(She throws back her head and opens her beak wide.)          CAW–W–W–W–W!

(The piece of cheese falls to the ground, right in front of Mr. Fox.)

**Mr. Fox:**
(Grabbing the cheese)

Thank you, Miss Crow! For giving me this excellent cheese, I will give you an excellent piece of advice:
Never believe flattery!

(He skips off, eating the cheese.)

**Narrator:**

So Miss Crow learned a very important lesson: Too much pride can make you look like a fool.

(Exits)

**Miss Crow:**
(Sits on the tree branch, looking sad—and hungry.)

**The End**

6. (Read the whole play at least one more time, calling on individual students to read.)
7. This time, I'll name students who will read the part for the different characters. (Assign a good reader to be the narrator:) [Student's name] will read all the things the narrator says.
• (Assign other students for the roles of stall keepers 1, 2, 3, Miss Crow, Mr. Fox.)

## Activity

1. (Direct and assist students in making or gathering modest props, stage settings and costumes.)
2. (Put on a reading version of the play for another group of students.)

# Grade 3 Literature

Grade 3 Literature contains 15 lessons, which are generally presented after every tenth lesson in the Reading strand. For each Literature lesson, students read one or two selections in the Literature Anthology and complete blackline masters from the Literature Guide. Lessons 5, 6, and 12 include read-to stories that appear in the Literature Guide.

| Lesson | Title | Author | Genre |
|---|---|---|---|
| 1 | *The Velveteen Rabbit* | Retold by Harriet Winfield | Modern fantasy |
| 2-1 | *Dreams* | Langston Hughes | Poem |
| 2-2 | *The Runner* | Faustin Charles | Poem |
| 3 | *The Emperor's New Clothes* | Retold by Harvey Cleaver | Fairy tale |
| 4 | *Why Leopard Has Black Spots* | Won-Ldy Paye | Folktale |
| 5-1 | *Boar Out There* | Cynthia Rylant | Realistic fiction |
| 5-2 | *Crossing the Creek* | Laura Ingalls Wilder | Read-to |
| 6-1 | *Camp on the High Prairie* | Laura Ingalls Wilder | Read-to |
| 6-2 | *Spaghetti* | Cynthia Rylant | Realistic fiction |
| 7 | *Charlie Best* | Ruth Corrin | Modern fantasy |
| 8 | *The Pancake Collector* | Jack Prelutsky | Poem |
| 9 | *Not Just Any Ring* | Danita Ross Haller | Realistic fiction |
| 10-1 | *A Lucky Thing* | Alice Schertle | Poem |
| 10-2 | *The New Kid* | Mike Makley | Poem |
| 11 | *Steps* | Deborah M. Newton Chocolate | Realistic fiction |
| 12-1 | *The Soup Stone* | Maria Leach | Folktale |
| 12-2 | *Julie Rescues Big Mack* | Roger Hall | Read-to |
| 13 | *Amelia Bedelia* | Peggy Parish | Humorous fiction |
| 14 | *My (Wow!) Summer Vacation* | Susan Cornell Poskanzer | Realistic fiction |
| 15 | *The Story of Daedalus and Icarus* | Fran Lehr | Play |

# Grade 4 Literature

Grade 4 Literature contains 12 stories, which are presented after every tenth lesson in the Reading strand. For each Literature lesson, students read a story in the Literature Anthology and complete pre-reading and post-reading activities.

| Lesson | Title | Author | Genre |
|--------|-------|--------|-------|
| 1 | *Hans in Luck* | Brothers Grimm | Folktale |
| 2 | *The Bracelet* | Yoshiko Uchida | Historical fiction |
| 3 | *The Jacket* | Steven Otfinoski | Modern fantasy |
| 4 | *Ginger's Challenge* | Josephine Noyes Felts | Animal story |
| 5 | *Brown Wolf* | Jack London | Classic short story |
| 6 | *Like Jake and Me* | Mavis Jukes | Realistic fiction |
| 7 | *Thank You, M'am* | Langston Hughes | Classic short story |
| 8 | *The Circuit* | Francisco Jiménez | Realistic fiction |
| 9 | *Salmon Count* | Clifford Trafzer | Historical fiction |
| 10 | *The No-Guitar Blues* | Gary Soto | Realistic fiction |
| 11 | *Raymond's Run* | Toni Cade Bambara | Sports story |
| 12 | *Without a Shirt* | Paul Jennings | Ghost story |

The following sample story from Grade 4, *Hans in Luck,* is presented after Lesson 10 in the Reading strand. Students begin the Literature lesson by completing several pre-reading activities. First they read vocabulary words that will appear in the story, along with their definitions. Then they read a Story Background passage that describes the origin of the story and important features of folktales. Finally, they read Focus Questions that they are to consider while reading the story.

After the pre-reading activities, students read the story aloud or silently. Then they complete one or more post-reading activities, including story questions, discussion topics, and writing assignments.

## Focus Questions

- What is the value of the exchanges that Hans makes, beginning with the lump of gold?
- Why are the people Hans meets so interested in making exchanges with him?
- How did Hans feel at the end of the story?
- Why do you think the story is titled "Hans in Luck"?

# Hans in Luck

### The Brothers Grimm

Illustrated by Allen Davis

---

**STORY 1**
**AFTER LESSON 10**

# Hans in Luck
### The Brothers Grimm

## New Vocabulary Words

1. exchange
2. peasant
3. fend

4. butcher
5. slaughter
6. remedy

7. trudge
8. vex
9. bargain
10. grindstone

## Definitions

1. When you **exchange** something, you trade one thing for another thing.
2. A **peasant** is a person who lives and works on a farm.
3. When you **fend** for yourself, you take care of yourself.
4. A **butcher** is a person who kills animals and cuts meat.
5. When people **slaughter** animals, they kill the animals.
6. A **remedy** is a solution to a problem.
7. A person who is **trudging** is walking in a tired way.
8. If a person is **vexed** with you, he or she is annoyed with you.
9. A **bargain** is a good deal.
10. A **grindstone** is a flat stone used to polish and sharpen blades.

## Story Background

"Hans in Luck" is a type of story called a folktale. Many folktales are old stories people told aloud. Parents would tell these stories to their children, and when the children became parents themselves, they would tell the same stories to their own children. Some stories were passed on in this way for hundreds of years without ever being written down.

In the early 1800s, two brothers from Germany named Jacob and Wilhelm Grimm began listening to folktales and writing them down. The folktales they collected were from Germany and other countries in Europe. Many of these folktales were hundreds of years old. In the folktale that you will read, Hans works as a servant for a master. Like many young people of that time, Hans had worked for his master for seven years. During that period, Hans had earned no money, but at the end of the seven years, his master pays Hans all his earnings in one payment. That payment is a lump of gold. The story tells what happens to Hans as he makes the long walk back to his mother's home with the lump of gold.

1

As Hans was trudging along, a man came riding by on a spirited horse, looking very lively. "Oh," cried Hans aloud, "how splendid riding must be! You sit at ease and don't stumble over stones."

The horseman heard Hans say this, and called out to him, "Well, what are you doing on foot?"

"I can't help myself," said Hans. "I have this great lump to carry. To be sure, it is gold, but then I can't hold my head straight because of it, and it hurts my shoulder."

"I'll tell you what," said the horseman, "we will trade. I will give you my horse, and you shall give me your lump of gold."

"Yes," said Hans. "But I warn you, you will find it heavy." And the horseman got down, took the gold, and, helping Hans up, he gave the reins into his hand. "When you want to go fast," said he, "you must click your tongue and cry 'Gee-up!'"

4

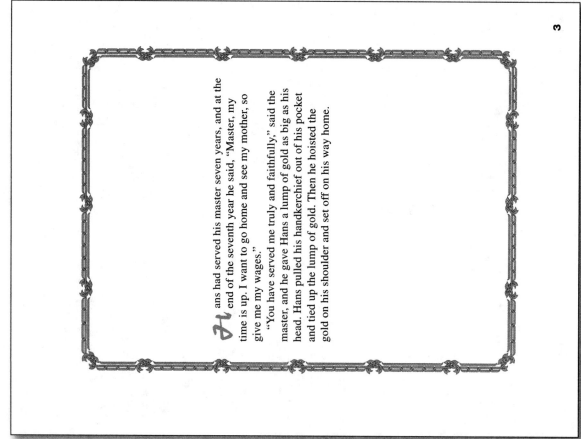

3

𝓗ans had served his master seven years, and at the end of the seventh year he said, "Master, my time is up. I want to go home and see my mother, so give me my wages."

"You have served me truly and faithfully," said the master, and he gave Hans a lump of gold as big as his head. Hans pulled his handkerchief out of his pocket and tied up the lump of gold. Then he hoisted the gold on his shoulder and set off on his way home.

Hans went along driving his cow quietly before him, and thinking all the while of the fine bargain he had made.

"With only a piece of bread I shall have everything I can possibly want, for I shall always be able to add butter and cheese to it. And if I am thirsty I have nothing to do but to milk my cow. What more is there for a heart to wish?"

And when he came to an inn he made a stop. He ate up all the food he had brought with him, and bought half a glass of milk with his last two pennies. Then he went on again, driving his cow toward the village where his mother lived.

It was now near the middle of the day, and the sun grew hotter and hotter. Hans began to feel very hot, and so thirsty that his tongue stuck to the roof of his mouth.

"Never mind," said Hans, "I can find a remedy. I will milk my cow at once." And tying her to a tree, and taking off his leather cap to serve for a pail, he began to milk, but not a drop came. And as he set to work rather awkwardly, the impatient beast gave him such a kick on the head with her hind foot that Hans fell to the ground. For some time he could not think where he was. Luckily a butcher came by wheeling along a young pig in a wheelbarrow.

6

And Hans, as he sat upon his horse, was glad at heart and rode off with merry cheer. After a while he thought he should like to go quicker, so he began to click with his tongue and to cry "Gee-up!" The horse began to trot, and Hans was thrown before he knew what was happening. There he lay in the ditch by the side of the road. The horse was caught by a peasant who was passing that way and driving a cow before him.

Hans pulled himself together and got upon his feet, feeling very vexed. "Riding is a poor business," said he, "especially on a mount like this, who starts off and throws you before you know where you are going. Never shall I try that game again. Now, your cow is something worth having. One can jog comfortably after her and have her milk, butter, and cheese every day, as part of the bargain. What would I not give to have such a cow!"

"Well now," said the peasant, "since it will be doing you such a favor, I don't mind exchanging my cow for your horse."

Hans agreed most joyfully, and the peasant, swinging himself into the saddle, was soon out of sight.

5

"This is terrible," cried the butcher, helping poor Hans on his legs again. Then Hans related to him all that had happened. The butcher handed him a jug of water, saying, "Here, take a drink, and you'll feel fine again. Of course the cow would give no milk, because she is old and only fit to pull burdens, or to be slaughtered."

"Well, to be sure," said Hans, scratching his head. "Who would have thought it? Of course it is a very handy way of getting meat when a man has a beast of his own to kill. But for my part I do not care much about beef, it is rather tasteless. Now, if I had but a young pig, that is much better meat, and then the sausages!"

"Look here, Hans," said the butcher, "just for love of you I will exchange. I will give you my pig instead of your cow."

"Heaven reward such kindness," cried Hans. Handing over the cow, he received in exchange the pig. The butcher lifted the pig out of the wheelbarrow and Hans led it away by a rope.

8

So on went Hans, thinking how everything turned out according to his wishes. After a while he met a peasant, who was carrying a fine white goose under his arm. They bid each other good-day, and Hans began to tell about his luck, and how he had made so many good exchanges. And the peasant told how he was taking the goose to a feast.

"Just feel how heavy it is," said the peasant, taking it up by the wings. "It has been fattening for the last eight weeks. When it is roasted, won't the fat run down."

"Yes, indeed," said Hans, weighing it in his hand, "very fine to be sure. But my pig is also desirable."

The peasant glanced cautiously on all sides of the animal and shook his head. "I am afraid," said he, "that there is something not quite right about your pig. In the village I have just left, a pig had actually been stolen from the sheriff's yard. I fear you have it in your hand. They have sent after the thief, and it would be a bad situation if the pig was found with you. At the least, they would throw you into a dark hole."

10

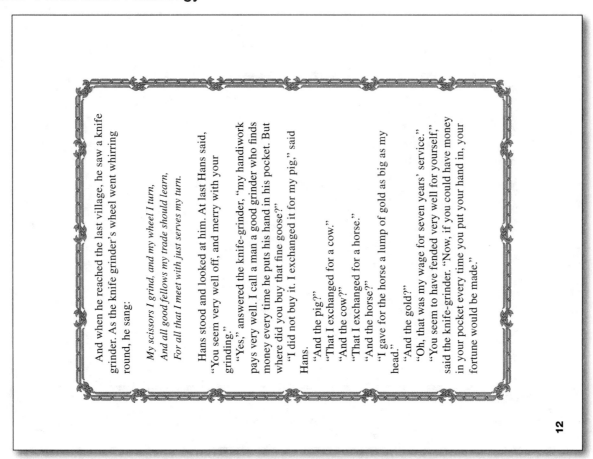

And when he reached the last village, he saw a knife grinder. As the knife grinder's wheel went whirring round, he sang:

*My scissors I grind, and my wheel I turn,*
*And all good fellows my trade should learn,*
*For all that I meet with just serves my turn.*

Hans stood and looked at him. At last Hans said, "You seem very well off, and merry with your grinding."

"Yes," answered the knife-grinder, "my handiwork pays very well. I call a man a good grinder who finds money every time he puts his hand in his pocket. But where did you buy that fine goose?"

"I did not buy it. I exchanged it for my pig," said Hans.

"And the pig?"

"That I exchanged for a cow."

"And the cow?"

"That I exchanged for a horse."

"And the horse?"

"I gave for the horse a lump of gold as big as my head."

"And the gold?"

"Oh, that was my wage for seven years' service."

"You seem to have fended very well for yourself," said the knife-grinder. "Now, if you could have money in your pocket every time you put your hand in, your fortune would be made."

12

Poor Hans grew pale with fright. "For heaven's sake," said he, "help me out of this scrape. I am a stranger in these parts. Take my pig and give me your goose."

"It will be running some risk," answered the man, "but I will do it so you won't experience grief." And so, taking the rope in his hand, he drove the pig quickly along a by-path, and lucky Hans went on his way home with the goose under his arm.

"The more I think of it," said he to himself, "the better the bargain seems. First I get the roast goose and then the fat. That will last a whole year for bread and dripping. And lastly, I can stuff my pillow with the beautiful white feathers. How comfortably I shall sleep upon my pillow, and how pleased my mother will be."

11

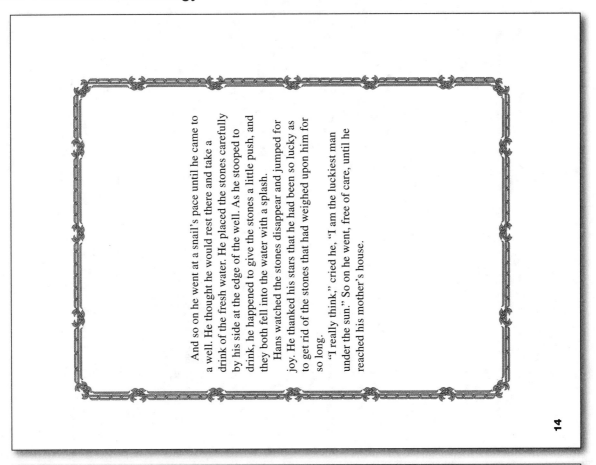

And so on he went at a snail's pace until he came to a well. He thought he would rest there and take a drink of the fresh water. He placed the stones carefully by his side at the edge of the well. As he stooped to drink, he happened to give the stones a little push, and they both fell into the water with a splash.

Hans watched the stones disappear and jumped for joy. He thanked his stars that he had been so lucky as to get rid of the stones that had weighed upon him for so long.

"I really think," cried he, "I am the luckiest man under the sun." So on he went, free of care, until he reached his mother's house.

14

13

"How shall I manage that?" said Hans.

"You must be a knife-grinder like me," said the man. "All you want is a grindstone, and the rest comes of itself. I have one here. To be sure, it is a little damaged, but I don't mind letting you have it in exchange for your goose. What do you say?"

"How can you ask?" answered Hans. "I shall be the luckiest fellow in the world. If I find money whenever I put my hand in my pocket, there is nothing more left to want."

And so he handed over the goose to the knife-grinder and received a grindstone in exchange.

"Now," said the knife-grinder, taking up a heavy common stone that lay near him, "here is another sort of stone that you can hammer out your old nails upon. Take it with you, and carry it carefully."

Hans lifted up the stone and carried it off with a contented mind. "I must have been born under a lucky star," cried he, while his eyes sparkled with joy. "I have only to wish for a thing and it is mine."

After a while he began to feel rather tired, because he had been on his legs since daybreak. He also began to feel rather hungry, for he had eaten up all he had. At last he could scarcely go on at all. He had to stop every few moments, for the stones weighed him down. He wished that he did not have to drag them along.

## Extending Comprehension

### Story Questions

1. Make a list of the exchanges Hans made, beginning with "He exchanged the lump of gold for a horse."
2. Tell why the people Hans met were so interested in making exchanges with him.
3. Why did Hans think exchanging the gold for the horse was a good idea?
4. Why did Hans feel lucky at the end of the story?
5. Why do you think the story is titled "Hans in Luck"?
6. What do you think Hans's mother said about his exchanges when he got home?

### Discussion Topics

1. This story can be interpreted in different ways. In one interpretation, Hans is unlucky because he keeps giving up valuable things until he ends up with nothing. In another interpretation, Hans is lucky because he gets rid of all the things that were a burden to him.

   Discuss these two interpretations with your classmates. During your discussion, try to answer the following questions:
   - Which interpretation do you agree with? Why?
   - Do you have another interpretation of the story? If so, what is it?
2. This story tells about people who make exchanges to get the things they want. With your classmates, discuss how you might get some things you want. During your discussion, try to answer the following questions:
   - What types of things would you like to get?
   - What kind of exchanges could you make to get those things?
3. People who are **gullible** believe everything they hear. It is easy to trick **gullible** people.

   With your classmates, decide if *gullible* is a word that you should use to describe Hans. During your discussion, try to answer the following questions:
   - Do the exchanges Hans makes make him appear gullible? Explain your answers.
   - Do Hans's statements make him sound gullible? Give some examples.

### Writing Ideas

1. Write out the conversation that Hans and his mother might have when Hans arrives home. Have Hans explain what happened on his journey. Tell what his mother says as she listens to his story.
2. Pretend that you could have any one of the things Hans had, including the lump of gold, the horse, the cow, the pig, the goose, the grindstone, or the freedom from care. Which would you choose? Explain what you would do with your choice. Tell why you chose that thing.

16

## Story 1

# *Hans in Luck*

## New Vocabulary Words

Everybody, take out your *Literature Anthology.* Turn to page 1. ✔
What is the title of this story? (Signal.) *"Hans in Luck."*
Who are the authors? (Signal.) *The Brothers Grimm.*
1. First we'll read some words from the story, and then we'll talk about what they mean.
2. Word 1 is **exchange.** What word? (Signal.) *Exchange.*
   • (Repeat for every numbered word.)
3. It's your turn to read all the words.
4. Word 1. What word? (Signal.) *Exchange.*
   • (Repeat for every numbered word.)

| | | |
|---|---|---|
| 1. exchange | 4. butcher | 7. trudge |
| 2. peasant | 5. slaughter | 8. vex |
| 3. fend | 6. remedy | 9. bargain |
| | | 10. grindstone |

## Definitions

(For each definition, call on a student to read the definition aloud; then, present the tasks for that definition to the group.)
1. *When you **exchange** something, you trade one thing for another thing.*
   • Everybody, what's another way of saying **Tricia traded her hair ribbon for a comb?** (Signal.) *Tricia exchanged her hair ribbon for a comb.*
2. *A **peasant** is a person who lives and works on a farm.*
   • Everybody, what do you call a person who lives and works on a farm? (Signal.) *A peasant.*
3. *When you **fend** for yourself, you take care of yourself.*
   • Here's another way of saying **The dog had to take care of himself: The dog had to fend for himself.**
   • Everybody, what's another way of saying **The dog had to take care of himself?** (Signal.) *The dog had to fend for himself.*
4. *A **butcher** is a person who kills animals and cuts meat.*
   • Everybody, what do you call a person who kills animals and cuts meat? (Signal.) *A butcher.*

5. When people **slaughter** animals, they kill the animals.
   - Everybody, what's another way of saying **The butcher killed the goat?** (Signal.) *The butcher slaughtered the goat.*
6. A **remedy** is a solution to a problem.
   - Everybody, what's another way of saying **Josef drank orange juice as a solution for his cold?** (Signal.) *Josef drank orange juice as a remedy for his cold.*
7. A person who is **trudging** is walking in a tired way.
   - Here's another way of saying **The dog walked home in a tired way: The dog trudged home.**
   - Everybody what's another way of saying **The dog walked home in a tired way?** (Signal.) *The dog trudged home.*
8. If a person is **vexed** with you, he or she is annoyed with you.
   - Everybody, what's another way of saying **Her mother was annoyed when Teresa spilled the soup?** (Signal.) *Her mother was vexed when Teresa spilled the soup.*
9. A **bargain** is a good deal.
   - When you make a bargain, you make a good deal.
   - What's another way of saying **Those blue jeans are a good deal?** (Signal.) *Those blue jeans are a bargain.*
10. A **grindstone** is a flat stone used to polish and sharpen blades.
    - Everybody, what is a flat stone used to polish and sharpen blades? (Signal.) *A grindstone.*

## Story Background

1. (Call on individual students to read two or three sentences.)
2. (After students complete a section, ask the questions for that section.)

---

"Hans in Luck" is a type of story called a folktale. Many folktales are old stories that people told aloud. Parents would tell these stories to their children, and when the children became parents themselves, they would tell same the stories to their own children. Some stories were passed on in this way for hundreds of years without ever being written down.

In the early 1800s, two brothers from Germany named Jacob and Wilhelm Grimm began listening to folktales and writing them down. The folktales they collected were from Germany and other countries in Europe. Many of these folktales were hundreds of years old.

---

- How did people pass on the folktales without writing them down? (Idea: *Parents told them to their children.*)
- About how long ago did the Brothers Grimm begin collecting folktales? (Idea: *About two hundred years ago.*)
- Where did those folktales come from? (Ideas: *Germany; other countries in Europe.*)

---

In the folktale you will read, Hans works as a servant for a master. Like many young people of that time, Hans had worked for his master for seven years. During that period, Hans had earned no money, but at the end of the seven years, his master pays Hans all his earnings in one payment. That payment is a lump of gold. The story tells what happens to Hans as he makes the long walk back to his mother's home with the lump of gold.

---

8    Grade 4 Literature Guide, Story 1

- Why did Hans receive a lump of gold? (Idea: *As payment for seven years of work.*)
- How long did Hans work before he got paid. (Signal.) *Seven years.*
- Why did Hans have to walk home? (Idea: *People didn't have cars, buses, or trains.*)
- What do you think might happen to Hans as he walks home? (Ideas: *People will try to steal the gold; he might get tired; he might lose the gold.*)

## Focus Questions

1. (Call on individual students to read the Focus Questions aloud.)
2. (Remind students to think about these questions as they read the story.)
   - *What is the value of the exchanges that Hans makes, beginning with the lump of gold?*
   - *Why are the people Hans meets so interested in making exchanges with him?*
   - *How did Hans feel at the end of the story?*
   - *Why do you think the story is titled "Hans in Luck"?*

**Hans in Luck**
by the Brothers Grimm

Illustrated by Allen Davis

Hans had served his master seven years, and at the end of the seventh year he said, "Master, my time is up. I want to go home and see my mother, so give me my wages."

"You have served me truly and faithfully," said the master, and he gave Hans a lump of gold as big as his head. Hans pulled his handkerchief out of his pocket and tied up the lump of gold. Then he hoisted the gold on his shoulder and set off on his way home.

As Hans was trudging along, a man came riding by on a spirited horse, looking very lively. "Oh," cried Hans aloud, "how splendid riding must be! You sit at ease and don't stumble over stones." The horseman heard Hans say this, and called out to him, "Well, what are you doing on foot?"

"I can't help myself," said Hans. "I have this great lump to carry. To be sure, it is gold, but then I can't hold my head straight because of it, and it hurts my shoulder."

"I'll tell you what," said the horseman, "we will trade. I will give you my horse, and you shall give me your lump of gold."

"Yes," said Hans. "But I warn you, you will find it heavy." And the horseman got down, took the gold, and, helping Hans up, he gave the reins into his hand.

"When you want to go fast," said he, "you must click your tongue and cry "'Gee-up!'"

And Hans, as he sat upon his horse, was glad at heart and rode off with merry cheer. After a while he thought he should like to go quicker, so he began to click with his tongue and to cry "Gee-up!" The horse began to trot, and Hans was thrown before he knew what was happening. There he lay in the ditch by the side of the road. The horse was caught by a peasant who was passing that way and driving a cow before him.

Hans pulled himself together and got upon his feet, feeling very vexed. "Riding is a poor business," said he, especially on a mount like this, who starts off and throws you before you know where you are going. Never shall I try that game again. Now, your cow

Grade 4 Literature Guide, Story 1    9

is something worth having. One can jog comfortably after her and have her milk, butter, and cheese every day, as part of the bargain. What would I not give to have such a cow!"

"Well now," said the peasant, "since it will be doing you such a favor, I don't mind exchanging my cow for your horse."

Hans agreed most joyfully, and the peasant, swinging himself into the saddle, was soon out of sight. Hans went along driving his cow quietly before him, and thinking all the while of the fine bargain he had made.

"With only a piece of bread I shall have everything I can possibly want, for I shall always be able to add butter and cheese to it. And if I am thirsty I have nothing to do but to milk my cow. What more is there for a heart to wish?"

And when he came to an inn he made a stop. He ate up all the food he had brought with him, and bought half a glass of milk with his last two pennies. Then he went on again, driving his cow toward the village where his mother lived.

It was now near the middle of the day, and the sun grew hotter and hotter. Hans began to feel very hot, and so thirsty that his tongue stuck to the roof of his mouth.

"Never mind," said Hans, "I can find a remedy. I will milk my cow at once." And tying her to a tree, and taking off his leather cap to serve for a pail, he began to milk, but not a drop came. And as he set to work rather awkwardly, the impatient beast gave him such a kick on the head with her hind foot that Hans fell to the ground. For some time he could not think where he was. Luckily a butcher came by wheeling along a young pig in a wheelbarrow.

"This is terrible," cried the butcher, helping poor Hans on his legs again. Then Hans related to him all that had happened. The butcher handed him a jug of water, saying, "Here, take a drink, and you'll feel fine again. Of course the cow would give no milk, because she is old and only fit to pull burdens, or to be slaughtered."

"Well, to be sure," said Hans, scratching his head. "Who would have thought it? Of course it is a very handy way of getting meat when a man has a beast of his own to kill. But for my part I do not care much about beef, it is rather tasteless. Now, if I had but a young pig, that is much better meat, and then the sausages!"

"Look here, Hans," said the butcher, "just for love of you I will exchange. I will give you my pig instead of your cow."

"Heaven reward such kindness," cried Hans. Handing over the cow, he received in exchange the pig. The butcher lifted the pig out of the wheelbarrow and Hans led it away by a rope.

So on went Hans, thinking how everything turned out according to his wishes. After a while he met a peasant, who was carrying a fine white goose under his arm. They bid each other good-day, and Hans began to tell about his luck, and how he had made so many good exchanges. And the peasant told how he was taking the goose to a feast.

"Just feel how heavy it is," said the peasant, taking it up by the wings. "It has been fattening for the last eight weeks. When it is roasted, won't the fat run down."

"Yes, indeed," said Hans, weighing it in his hand, "very fine to be sure. But my pig is also desirable."

The peasant glanced cautiously on all sides of the animal and shook his head. "I am afraid," said he, "that there is something not quite right about your pig. In the village I have just left, a pig had actually been stolen from the sheriff's yard. I fear you have it in your hand. They have sent after the thief, and it would be a bad situation if the pig was found with you. At the least, they would throw you into a dark hole."

Poor Hans grew pale with fright. "For heaven's sake," said he, "help me out of this scrape. I am a stranger in these parts. Take my pig and give me your goose."

"It will be running some risk," answered the man, "but I will do it so you won't experience grief." And so, taking the rope in his hand, he drove the pig quickly along a by-path, and lucky Hans went on his way home with the goose under his arm.

"The more I think of it," said he to himself, "the better the bargain seems. First I get the roast goose and then the fat. That will last a whole year for bread and dripping. And lastly, I can stuff my pillow with the beautiful white feathers. How comfortably I shall sleep upon my pillow, and how pleased my mother will be."

And when he reached the last village, he saw a knife grinder. As the knife grinder's wheel went whirring round, he sang:

<blockquote>
My scissors I grind, and my wheel I turn,<br>
And all good fellows my trade should learn,<br>
For all that I meet with just serves my turn.
</blockquote>

Hans stood and looked at him. At last Hans said, "You seem very well off, and merry with your grinding."

"Yes," answered the knife-grinder, "my handiwork pays very well. I call a man a good grinder who finds money every time he puts his hand in his pocket. But where did you buy that fine goose?"

"I did not buy it. I exchanged it for my pig," said Hans.

"And the pig?"

"That I exchanged for a cow."

"And the cow?"

"That I exchanged for a horse."

"And the horse?"

"I gave for the horse a lump of gold as big as my head."

"And the gold?"

"Oh, that was my wage for seven years' service."

"You seem to have fended very well for yourself," said the knife-grinder. "Now, if you could have money in your pocket every time you put your hand in, your fortune would be made."

"How shall I manage that?" said Hans.

"You must be a knife-grinder like me," said the man. "All you want is a grindstone, and the rest comes of itself. I have one here. To be sure, it is a little damaged, but I don't mind letting you have it in exchange for your goose. What do you say?"

"How can you ask?" answered Hans. "I shall be the luckiest fellow in the world. If I find money whenever I put my hand in my pocket, there is nothing more left to want."

And so he handed over the goose to the knife-grinder and received a grindstone in exchange.

"Now," said the knife-grinder, taking up a heavy common stone that lay near him, "here is another sort of stone that you can hammer out your old nails upon. Take it with you, and carry it carefully."

Hans lifted up the stone and carried it off with a contented mind. "I must have been born under a lucky star," cried he, while his eyes sparkled with joy. "I have only to wish for a thing and it is mine."

After a while he began to feel rather tired, because he had been on his legs since daybreak. He also began to feel rather hungry, for he had eaten up all he had. At last he could scarcely go on at all. He had to stop every few moments, for the stones weighed him down. He wished that he did not have to drag them along.

And so on he went at a snail's pace until he came to a well. He thought he would rest there and take a drink of the fresh water. He placed the stones carefully by his side at the edge of the well. As he stooped to drink, he happened to give the stones a little push, and they both fell into the water with a splash.

Hans watched the stones disappear and jumped for joy. He thanked his stars that he had been so lucky as to get rid of the stones that had weighed upon him for so long.

"I really think," cried he, "I am the luckiest man under the sun." So on he went, free of care, until he reached his mother's house.

## Extending Comprehension

(The following Extending Comprehension activities can be presented after students finish reading the story. The activities also appear in the *Literature Anthology*.)

1. (Students can answer the Story Questions either orally or in writing. If the questions are presented orally, use the script below.)
2. (Students can select one or more Discussion Topics. Discussions can take place in small groups or with the entire class.)
3. (Students can use the Writing Ideas to respond to the story in writing.)

## Story Questions

1. Make a list of the exchanges Hans made, beginning with "He exchanged the lump of gold for a horse."
   - (List: *He exchanged the lump of gold for a horse, the horse for a cow, the cow for a pig, the pig for a goose, the goose for a grindstone, and the grindstone for freedom from cares.*)
2. Tell why the people Hans met were so interested in making exchanges with him.
   - (Ideas: *Because they wanted what he had; because they got good bargains; because it was easy to talk him into an exchange.*)
3. Why did Hans think exchanging the gold for the horse was a good idea?
   - (Ideas: *Because the gold was heavy; because he could ride the horse.*)
4. Why did Hans feel lucky at the end of the story?
   - (Ideas: *Because he was free of care; because he made so many bargains on his journey; because he had gotten rid of the heavy stones; because he was almost home.*)

5. Why do you think the story is titled "Hans in Luck"?
   - (Ideas: *Because Hans thought he was lucky; because the author is making fun of Hans.*)
6. What do you think Hans's mother said about his exchanges when he got home?
   - (Ideas: *I'm so glad to see you; where is your payment for seven years' work? Accept all other reasonable responses.*)

## Discussion Topics

1. This story can be interpreted in different ways. In one interpretation, Hans is unlucky because he keeps giving up valuable things until he ends up with nothing. In another interpretation, Hans is lucky because he gets rid of all the things that were a burden to him. Discuss these two interpretations with your classmates. During your discussion, try to answer the following questions:
   - Which interpretation do you agree with? Why?
   - Do you have another interpretation of the story? If so, what is it?
2. This story tells about people who make exchanges to get the things they want. With your classmates, discuss how you might get some things you want. During your discussion, try to answer the following questions:
   - What types of things would you like to get?
   - What kind of exchanges could you make to get those things?
3. People who are **gullible** believe everything they hear. It is easy to trick **gullible** people. With your classmates, decide if **gullible** is a word that you should use to describe Hans. During your discussion, try to answer the following questions:
   - Do the exchanges Hans makes make him appear *gullible?* Explain your answers.
   - Do Hans's statements make him sound *gullible?* Give some examples.

## Writing Ideas

1. Write out the conversation that Hans and his mother might have when Hans arrives home. Have Hans explain what happened on his journey. Tell what his mother says as she listens to his story.
2. Pretend that you could have any one of the things Hans had, including the lump of gold, the horse, the cow, the pig, the goose, the grindstone, or freedom from care. Which would you choose? Explain what you would do with your choice. Tell why you chose that thing.

## Grade 5 Literature

Grade 5 Literature contains 12 stories, which are presented after every tenth lesson in the Reading strand. For each Literature lesson, students read a story in the Literature Anthology and complete pre-reading and post-reading activities.

| Lesson | Title | Author | Genre |
|:---:|---|---|---|
| 1 | *Why Bush Cow and Elephant Are Bad Friends* | Ashley Bryan | Folktale |
| 2 | *Blue Willow* | Pam Conrad | Legend |
| 3 | *In the Middle of the Night* | Philippa Pearce | Classic short story |
| 4 | *The Shrinking of Treehorn* | Florence Parry Heide | Modern fantasy |
| 5 | *The Gallant Tailor* | Brothers Grimm | Folktale |
| 6 | *Shrewd Todie and Lyzer the Miser* | Isaac Bashevis Singer | Classic short story |
| 7 | *No One is Going to Nashville* | Mavis Jukes | Realistic fiction |
| 8 | *Barn Gravity* | Nancy Springer | Animal story |
| 9 | *The Gold Cadillac* | Mildred Taylor | Historical fiction |
| 10 | *The Hope Bakery* | Tim Wynne-Jones | Realistic fiction |
| 11 | *Trick-or-Treating* | Gary Soto | Modern fantasy |
| 12 | *Willie and the Christmas Spruce* | Larry Bograd | Realistic fiction |